CAUTIONS FOR THOSE
WHO HEAR GOD'S VOICE

GOD TALK

RUTH A. TUCKER

An imprint of InterVarsity Press
Downers Grove, Illinois

To

John W. Worst

Beloved husband and best friend

for insights and challenges as we grapple with God

and all things incomprehensible

InterVarsity Press
P.O. Box 1400, Downers Grove, IL 60515-1426
World Wide Web: www.ivpress.com
E-mail: mail@ivpress.com

InterVarsity Press® is the book-publishing division of InterVarsity Christian Fellowship/USA®, a student movement active on campus at hundreds of universities, colleges and schools of nursing in the United States of America, and a member movement of the International Fellowship of Evangelical Students. For information about local and regional activities, write Public Relations Dept., InterVarsity Christian Fellowship/USA, 6400 Schroeder Rd., P.O. Box 7895, Madison, WI 53707-7895, or visit the IVCF website at <www.intervarsity.org>.

Design: Matt Smith

ISBN 10: 0-8308-3331-5
ISBN 13: 978-0-8308-3331-3

Printed in the United States of America ∞

Library of Congress Cataloging-in-Publication Data

Tucker, Ruth, 1945-
God talk: cautions for those who hear God's voice / Ruth A. Tucker.
p. cm.
Includes bibliographical references and index.
ISBN 0-8308-3331-5 (pbk.: alk. paper)
1. Spiritual life—Christianity. 2. Silence—Religious aspects—Christianity. 3. Hidden God. I. Title.
BV4509.5.T83 2006
248.4—dc22

2005029023

P 18 17 16 15 14 13 12 11 10 9 8 7 6 5 4 3 2 1
Y 18 17 16 15 14 13 12 11 10 09 08 07 06 05

CONTENTS

INTRODUCTION

[Talking to God is] like picking up the phone and recognizing the voice of your best friend.

LOREN CUNNINGHAM, *IS THAT REALLY YOU, GOD?*

God, are you listening? Did you get my message? Will you ever call back? For some people these are haunting questions. We so easily pick up the phone and dial someone across the street or halfway around the world, but God cannot be reached. Are we supposed to be on talking terms with God? Is the One we worship a conversational God? Is talking to God like talking to my best friend? Or is it like talking to myself? With a preponderance of books on *listening* to God in recent years, many people are left thinking that either they have dialed the wrong number or the phone to the throne has been disconnected. It sometimes seems as though God oversees a colossal, cosmic answering machine out there somewhere in the heavens, and we, the gadget-challenged earthlings, have been put on hold listening to eternal elevator music.

I do not have a Type P personality—as in phone. In my home I have one functioning telephone: no cell phone, no fax, no voicemail, no answering machine. I don't even have touch-tone, which saves me $2.43 a month on my local bill. When I make calls, my preference is a live voice—a person over a recording—except when I need to know store hours or some other general information. If I leave a message, chances are the other party calls back when I'm away or simply doesn't return the call at all.

For some people, communicating with God is equally frustrating; it's as difficult as touch-toning your way through a complicated corporate phone matrix. And the phones themselves are often complex, with instructions that are convoluted at best. Indeed, after purchasing a cell phone, a person is expected to master the directions before making that first call. And making the call is the easiest part. I was recently vacationing with a friend who spent hours, of what should have been leisure time, trying to retrieve messages on her cell phone. She returned home from vacation unsuccessful. So also with God. We go through life with unretrieved messages—unable to make sense out of the directions. How-to prayer manuals are plentiful. Some are vague; others are unequivocal, telling us that before we even pick up the receiver we should master the instructions or at least be in a meditative mood or have all our sins confessed.

GOD AND PRIVATE PRAYER

Is it possible, I wonder, in this overly communicative Western culture, that we are expecting too much from God? Just like our best friend with a cell phone, we expect God to *pick up* every time we call. And we make those calls at an ever-increasing rate. "Those cell phones we see everywhere," writes Louis Rene Beres in a June 2005 editorial in the *Chicago Tribune,* "are no more or less than a desperate attempt to keep from being alone with ourselves in a vast, uncaring universe" ("Don't Hang Up," June 12, 2005). Indeed, it's almost impossible to read a newspaper while waiting for a connection at O'Hare airport or to take a leisurely walk along the Grand River without hearing someone mindlessly yakking on a cell phone. Does this phenomenon parallel our own attempts to communicate with God? And is our communication frequently self-serving? Our reported words from God often sound eerily like our own. God's opinions and priorities are ours, and we expect customer care. Just as we pick up the phone or go online to order from a garden or fashion catalog, we dial a prayer and God becomes yet another mail-order outlet.

Who is God, and how does God relate to us? This is a difficult question because the answer is typically based primarily on our own experience. Relationships with God are perceived as *intimate*. The *me*-focus permeates contemporary spirituality as each person communicates privately with God. Subjective encounters with God are to be taken at face value and not subjected to theological review. Challenging someone's spiritual experience is considered off-limits in nice company.

Recently, I was with friends in Denver. There were four of us sitting around a dinette table having lunch. "Tell Freda about your new book," Darlene urged me. So I introduced the topic of the silence of God. Within minutes we were on the subject of prayer, and in the course of our conversation I told about a public testimony of answered prayer that I had heard many years ago. I was then teaching at Grand Rapids School of the Bible and Music, and every Monday we had "report chapel." Students or faculty would stand up and share ministry experiences, answered prayer or prayer requests. A young man stood and shared God's answer to his prayer to not let it rain. He had spent the weekend at Lake Michigan with a youth group, and he told how, in answer to his prayer, God gave them sunshine the entire time—not a cloud in the sky. I cringed as I listened. West Michigan had been enduring a prolonged dry spell, and we desperately needed rain. To be fair, the young man was from out of state and may not have been aware of the severe drought, but the point I was making to my friends over lunch was that we should be cautious about making such claims for answered prayer.

Freda strongly disagreed. In fact, she had an answered *rain prayer* on the tip of her tongue. She reported how she had taken her grandchildren to play miniature golf, and it started to rain just as they were arriving. Her young grandson announced that he was going to pray that God would stop the rain long enough for them to play eighteen holes. As

Freda tells the story, the rain stopped long enough for them to complete their round, and it started up again as soon as they were finished. In her mind it was God's way of making himself real to her grandson.

Now, I realize there is no way to counter answered prayer, but I did challenge Freda, wondering if we really should want our grandchildren or anyone else to have that image of God—one who holds back the rain for us to play golf. Is God then like a genie in a bottle, ready to do our bidding? And I asked about the little boy who arrived to play golf as they were leaving. Did God dump on him just because he didn't say a prayer?

It was an animated discussion, and Kathy was the next one to offer a personal testimony. A graduate of Moody Bible Institute, Kathy was nurtured in a mentality of asking God for specific needs, particularly money, which is a common need of college students. She was going through some tight financial times, and she prayed that God would provide $1,000. Only days later in the mail she received an envelope with a letter from the IRS and a bill for $1,000. "You mean a check," Darlene interjected. "No, I mean a *bill!*" Kathy insisted. "The IRS was claiming I owed $1,000!" For Kathy, it was like "a slap in the face," and it led to a difficult time for her spiritually.

The conversation with my friends moved away from the table on to the sofa and easy chairs, while Darlene got out her well-worn Bible, and we talked for most of two hours about God, silence and prayer. We ended as four friends with four different perspectives—much as we had started—but we affirmed, each to a varying degree, that God does indeed answer prayer, though not necessarily immediately or audibly, and that he answers most often through secondary or ordinary means.

FILLING THE VOID

The setting for this book is a spherical rock orbiting a star in a small solar system on the edge of a rather nondescript galaxy—one of a hundred billion or so in an expanding universe. The date is fifteen billion years—give or take a few billion—after the big bang.

In *Repetition,* Søren Kierkegaard's hero laments:

> One sticks one's finger into the soil to tell by the smell in what land one is: I stick my finger in existence—it smells of nothing. Where am I? Who am I? How came I here? What is this thing called the world? What does this world mean? Who is it that has lured me into the world? Why was I not consulted? . . . How did I obtain an interest in this big enterprise they call reality? . . . And if I am to be compelled to take part in it, where is the director? I should like to make a remark to him. Is there no director? Whither shall I turn with my complaint?

The incomprehensible size and distance of the universe combined with the transcendence of God easily causes a mere human to seem utterly insignificant. Science, with every passing day, pushes the edges of the universe—and God—further and further away. Why then doesn't God break through and say something that will startle us and assure us, scientists and all, that he is really there?

Silence, particularly when it erupts where sound is supposed to be, is troubling. This can be most uncomfortable especially if God is involved. Indeed, the silence of God can be most disquieting. And in our current age, as the distance between the human and divine seems to expand with the universe so does the temptation to fill the space with noise and chatter. This craving for sound—sound of any kind—is natural. In a contemporary evangelical worship service, the audible (whether music, hand clapping, preaching or praying) greatly outweighs the silent (silent prayer, the moment of silence, the slight pauses between worship elements). And this craving for sound, for works, for noise has its counterpart in literature. In Baroque poetry, for example, one finds "a great flood of metaphors and symbols" in a grasping attempt "to keep open the avenues of communication between man and God." (How different was the more spiritually secure poetry of the high Renaissance in which "God is both transcendent and immanent.") But in the end it failed. Baroque art represented the same expression of separation from God—expressions that sought to fill vacuous religiosity with the wordiness of God.

There is a similar spirituality today, perhaps aggravated by the Hubble telescope phenomenon. That piece of technology is truly one of the great marvels of this generation. But it frustrates as much as it fascinates. It captured the headlines during Earth's close encounter with Mars—coming closer than it has in many thousands of years. And Hubble's cameras snapped it all. But more than mapping Mars, Hubble documents deep-space distance before our very eyes. So much so that we have become anesthetized to the fact that *out there* are billions and billions and billions—of space, nothingness, chaos, destruction. One space story recently reported that big galaxies are *gobbling* smaller ones. How insignificant we are in comparison. Despite Carl Sagan's enthusiastic sense of discovery that made it all sound reasonable, it is too much to grasp. A numbness sets in. We are forced to comprehend what is incomprehensible.

Is it possible that we are filling our own sense of silence and void with a projected wordiness of God? There are countless books and tapes and seminars on hearing God's voice, listening to God and having two-way conversations in prayer. Are these indicative of a collective craving for special words and messages—messages transmitted randomly to people in their prayer closets or driving home from work?

Is there perhaps another perspective: one that offers a deeper comprehension and confidence in God than those that are dependent on subjective and individualized testimonials of divine intervention and communication?

EMBRACING GOD'S SILENCE

The uniqueness of this book is its *celebration* of God's silence, or if not that, at least a sense of security in God's silence. Much has been written on the silence of God, but most often with a sigh of resignation—as though the silence is something that we endure. Here I maintain that silence is better than speaking if for no other reason than the fact that silence is far less open to misinterpretation and disagreement than is the spoken word. When God is silent, no one can claim to be God's spokesperson and interpret for God. We too must be silent, and that's not all bad.

Most people regard God's silence as though it were the *silent treatment*. It is not. It is surely no sign of passive-aggressive behavior. God's silence is neither good nor bad. It simply *is*. Silence is an *attribute*—or an *attitude*—of God, and for that reason, even as I worship God, I acknowledge God's silence. I not only acknowledge God's silence, but I also cultivate my own spiritual journey in light of it. I take God's silence seriously, but at the same time I am often amused and even humored by this silent One who has far more than our little solar system *in his hands*.

Another important aspect of this book is its focus on two genres of writing that are rarely brought together in the same context. I refer to them separately as the literature of *listening* and literature of *lament*. The former includes the mystics throughout the ages, but I focus primarily on contemporary evangelicals who speak and write about a talkative God. The latter are more likely mainline Protestants and Catholics whose lament over God's absence and silence is sometimes related to personal sorrow. This literature, though often from a different perspective than mine, has provided substance and support for some of my tenuous conclusions.

This book affirms three primary propositions that emerge repeatedly. The first is that apparent experiences of interactive supernatural communication with God should not be perceived as a higher way or deeper spirituality. Those who do not testify to such intimate conversations with God are often made to feel as though they are lesser Christians—ones who are missing out on a higher level of spirituality that is available simply for the asking. Unlike some religions, Christianity does not promote the concept of tiers of spirituality that afford those on the highest level a unique capability to converse with God.

The second proposition is that there are negative side effects to this sort of interactive personalized spirituality. Such a spiritual perspective too easily humanizes God, whose voice often begins to sound very much like our own. It fails to recognize our own subjectivity and self-absorption. It tends to focus more on the individual than on God—or on the community. It easily lends itself to spiritual abuse (as in "I prayed about this decision"; therefore, it's right). And it opens itself to elitism—a favored friendship with God (as is true in everyday name-dropping, when people reference their familiarity with the rich and famous).

The third proposition that repeatedly emerges is that there is a time-tested, biblical "middle way" that affirms neither a garrulous God nor a distant deity. It recognizes God's sovereignty in the universe whose *distance* and *absence* is ameliorated by the incarnate Christ, who lived and walked among us, was crucified, died and rose from the grave, leaving behind the Spirit who guides us in all truth, the very Word of God—the silent Word of God. This recognition of God's silence should not be seen as a step backward, a move toward *liberalism* or worldliness. Indeed, I will argue that the talkative God of today is a second-rate version of the trinitarian God, who as Father spoke in times past, who as Son incarnate lived among us, and who as Spirit inspired and illumines the Scriptures, the silent Word of God.

I have no doubt that this volume is potentially controversial. Not so much because it challenges cherished beliefs, but far more so because it challenges cherished beliefs on matters of *spirituality*—such things as prayer and listening to God and God's speaking to us. The field of spiritual formation is one of the most rapidly expanding disciplines in theological education today. But very little is written to stir discussion and debate, except for some rare books like Mike Yaconelli's *Messy Spirituality.* The subject of spirituality is imbued with a sacred quality, and criticism is out of line.

The first chapters focus on the perceived *voice* of God in the public realm, in the church (institutional and otherwise) and in the apologetical defense of the faith. Chapter four examines what Scripture says about the silence of God as well as Scripture as the voice of God. The following three chapters focus on the will of God, learning to listen to God and private two-way prayer. Chapter eight tackles the matter of anger, lament and the hopeless sense of absence; chapter nine examines the incarnation, and the final chapter seeks to show how the Christian can find solace and security in God's silence.

The scope of the volume is much broader than merely God-talk or God-silence. Indeed, my primary focus is on humans, not God. The book strikes a cautionary tone in the subtitle: "Don't be too sure about hearing the voice of God; God often resides and responds in silence." As such, the subject is wide-ranging, from matters of prayer and miracles to politics and apologetics, with biblical and theological reflections.

In researching this topic I have spent many hours on the Internet. One site particularly intrigued me. The subtitle was "Hearing the Voice of God at Wal-Mart." I clicked on, thinking I had found a testimonial that might be the missing clue to this mystery. Alas, all I found was how to buy a book titled *Hearing the Voice of God*—at Wal-Mart. Websites abound on the matter of the silence of God, but even more common are websites featuring special messages from God and how to hear the voice of God. What is rarely found on websites or in books is patient acceptance of God's silence.

As one who has never *heard* the voice of God as a direct form of communication, I take solace in the silence of God. I embrace the Bible as God's special revelation, and from the Bible I draw comfort, guidance and principles for living. But for many people that is not enough. God's message, in order to be personal, must be more than what is written on the pages of Scripture.

In affirming God's silence I do not mean to, in any sense, dismiss

God's *presence.* The presence of God is more mysterious than the speaking of God. God's presence adds nothing to Scripture that has not already been spoken, and when it is truly felt it is not something easily put into words. Nevertheless, God's presence is most often understood in stories.

My friend and former student, Sharon Bytwerk, told such a story in a recent chapel service. Eight years ago, she and her husband were hosting a Calvin College semester-abroad program. Their two children, David in tenth grade and Kate in seventh, had come with them. One weekend they went hiking in a mountainous region in Slovakia. It was there on a foggy morning that Kate, who had gone out for a short walk, disappeared. After three hours of searching, a call came that she had fallen and had been found, still conscious, by some Czech hikers who transported her to a hospital. When Sharon and Randy arrived, they were told she was sleeping—a condition perhaps brought on by sedatives. The next morning she awakened and recognized them, but by afternoon she had slipped into a coma from which she never awoke.

> By evening, when Randy was on the phone to the embassy, I found myself getting up and going to the bathroom-cleaning closet. . . . I had to battle with God. I was desperate. . . . I would wrestle with God, and just as Jacob got his blessing, I would get Kate. . . . I tantrumed like a two-year-old on that bathroom floor. Pounding my fist. . . . In the midst of that I had the experience of Kate's voice, "Mom, can I go?" I also had the phrase, "Let God be God." Both phrases bumping in my head. I wanted to yell NO. You don't know! And immediately I thought of the Father giving up his Son for me. I knew. I was being called to open my fist. And I did. I went back to Kate's room. It was the hardest and easiest thing I have ever done. Everything was the same, and everything was very different. Kate still lay in a coma. I told her, "Honey, if God says you can go, you go. And have fun. We're going to let God call the shots. . . . But

> if Jesus says you can come back I would like to have you come back." . . . That was all. And the peace that flooded me is *beyond all understanding*. As I sat at her bedside I began to sing, one of the songs was "Beautiful Savior." Kate died.
>
> Six months later, we were back in the States, one night *anger* welled up in me. It was—*not fair.* It was God's fault Kate died, and I didn't want him as my God anymore. I went up to our bedroom. I told him what I had decided. . . . Within seconds, I was *terrified.* I had lived six months without Kate, but I couldn't live one second without God. I *begged* him to forgive me. I begged and repented over and over. And *again I felt his arms around me*. That bitter anger has not returned. Since Kate's death, he has become *so real*. He is more important to me than life.

Sharon's is a story of God's presence. It stands alone—and yet it speaks to everyone who searches for God. This is not a heartwarming story of God telling me which detour to take so that I don't miss my appointment. No this is a story of *real* presence that has no explanation apart from the profound and mysterious love of God.

This book comes from one who is on a spiritual pilgrimage, seeking to know Christ and the power of his resurrection and the fellowship of sharing in his sufferings. Though I feel safe in the silence of God, I am in another sense searching for God—surely I am not one who knows and then passes along all the answers. The words of Parker Palmer are mine:

> It is a mistake to imagine that writers are experts on the things they write about—at least, it is a mistake in my case! I write about things I am still wrestling with, things that are important to me but that I have not yet figured out. . . . I write to explore vexing questions and real dilemmas, to take myself into territories I have never seen before in hopes of understanding myself and the world a bit better.

1

HEAVEN'S MEGAPHONE

God Speaks in the Public Square

I think George Bush is going to win in a walk. . . . I really believe I'm hearing from the Lord it's going to be like a blowout election in 2004. It's shaping up that way.

PAT ROBERTSON

There are countless pastors who testify of God *speaking* to them to leave one church and accept a *call* to another—and, perhaps only coincidentally, to a larger and more prestigious one. And there are people who claim that God tells them which store to shop at and what movie to see. If God intervenes with special messages about relatively inconsequential matters, should we be surprised if God speaks to others about very significant events?

> "America Attacked Iraq, Because God Told George Bush To"
>
> No, it wasn't the Weapons of Mass Destruction and it wasn't those United Nations resolutions either. Those aluminum tubes had nothing to do with it and neither did Iraq's terrorist connections. God told George Bush to Attack Iraq.
>
> Never mind that thousands and thousands of innocent people were killed by our forces and who really cares if little kids are dying from disease, because George Bush's God said that all of that was OK.

I found the above excerpt on the Internet. Much of what we find on the Web is unreliable, and I personally doubt that President George W. Bush has ever claimed that God told him to bomb Baghdad. In fact, most people, including most Christians, would be very suspicious about any claims of God *speaking* to an American president and telling him how to conduct foreign policy. But why not? Shouldn't we expect it? Shouldn't we assume God is speaking and that either the president is not listening or is defying the message, or that he is following the specific instructions? Or is God silent in such situations?

THE GOD OF INCONSEQUENTIALS

I recently read a one-page feature in *Guideposts* magazine titled "What Prayer Can Do: Power in Our Day-to-Day Lives." Here Rebecca Roberts says that as a child her grandmother taught her to make lace. But as an adult with a family she "set tatting aside." Years later, after her grandmother had died, "she spent an entire morning trying to tat" but "ended up with nothing more than a tangled mess of knots." She threw down the shuttle, ready to give up.

> *Lord,* I prayed: *Grandma is gone now. Please don't let me lose what she taught me too.*
>
> Just then a small voice seemed to whisper, "You've got to flip it, Becky."
>
> It all came back in a rush. I flipped the piece around and started looping a knot, then another. They formed a ring. Once again I was making lace.

Whether or not God intervened and told Rebecca how to tat is impossible to verify and is relatively inconsequential, except perhaps to Rebecca. No one is going to get worked up over one woman's tatting. Yet the story is offered as an example of prayer *power.*

But what if God told President Bush to bomb North Korea or Iran? If

God is going to intervene in human affairs and speak, George W. Bush would qualify as one who deals with weighty matters. In Scripture, God never intervened in tatting. But God did tell rulers to wipe out their enemies. Has God changed? Many people testify how God speaks to them today. Others write books on how to listen to God. But the message received is invariably something inconsequential. Why? Because tatting is not controversial. God is allowed to speak on such things. But God is not permitted to speak on war and other weighty matters. Have we fashioned for ourselves a domesticated, talking god of tatting? Such is not the God of Scripture.

God either intervenes and speaks today or God does not. To argue that God intervenes in tatting but not bombing simply will not do.

This God of inconsequentials is a relatively recent invention. Before our era of democracy, political polling and political correctness, leaders claimed to be acting on God's commands. Constantine's victory at Milvian Bridge in A.D. 312 was a result, he claimed, of his prayer to the "Supreme God." The answer came in the form of a cross above the sun in the noonday sky, with the words, "Conquer by this." This was, by Constantine's own account, the occasion of his conversion to Christianity.

Pope Urban II, likewise, did not think God silent in matters of military prowess and foreign policy. In 1095, he preached an open-air sermon in a town in southern France. His words were chilling: "From the confines of Jerusalem and from the city of Constantinople a horrible tale has gone forth. . . . An accursed race, a race utterly alienated from God . . . has invaded the lands of those Christians and depopulated them by the sword, plundering and fire." The pitch of his voice swelled as he recounted the atrocities, and the crowd became more and more agitated. Then he implored the dignitaries and destitute alike with a ringing summons: "Start upon the road to the Holy Sepulchre, to tear that land from the wicked race and subject it to yourselves." A spontaneous cry arose from the crowd, *Deus Vult! Deus Vult!* ("God wills it"). With that sermon the First

Crusade was launched by the pope, with the battle cry *Deus Vult!*

Today church historians as well as ordinary Christians almost universally condemn the Crusades, an expression of regret given legs in 2000, by way of the Reconciliation Walk—a Christian pilgrimage in the steps of the Crusaders, asking forgiveness along the way. But what about *Deus Vult,* God's will? Has God changed his mind? Pope Urban's God was not silent.

Joan of Arc did not believe God to be silent on major military and political matters. As a teenager (in the 1420s) she began hearing voices. God, she was convinced, was speaking to her through Saint Michael, Saint Catherine and Saint Margaret—calling her to lead the armies of France against the English occupiers. Her leadership in the political and military realm is rife with legend, but there is no story at all without the voice of God. And in the end, in the midst of political intrigue, this voice was deemed demonic, and she was burned at the stake—only to be posthumously judged not guilty a quarter century later and canonized a saint in 1920.

Like the French lass, Oliver Cromwell did not presume God was silent on matters of military exploit. In 1649, after capturing the seaport town of Drogheda and massacring its residents, Cromwell, who was then Lord Protector of England, celebrated the "righteous judgment of God upon these barbarous [Irish] wretches."

Closer to home, Jonathan Edwards, the renowned American preacher and theologian, believed that through prayer God was defeating the antichrist (the pope) and his "popish" military forces. According to George Marsden, Edwards called for the "Concert of Prayer," which he believed would serve to usher in the millennium. For Edwards, religious awakenings and military victories were melded together in God's millennial designs. When British forces defeated French forces, it was because "God gave into our hands" the fort at Cape Breton, which was, according to Edwards, "a dispensation of providence, the most remarkable in its kind, that has been in many ages, and a great evidence of God's being one that hears prayer." Charles Chauncy, another New England preacher, went even further in his assessment: "I scarce know of a conquest since the days of Joshua and Judges, wherein the finger of God is more visible." But God's work against the Catholics was not only evident in battles. It was seen when God (by means of lightning), according to Edwards, burned a Jesuit library—"one of the best-chosen . . . in Europe."

There were ministers and ordinary citizens who were skeptical about the notion of God's direct answers to prayer in such events. Some lampooned Edwards, the most vocal of whom was Benjamin Franklin. Mocking New England piety, he wrote: "Some seem to think forts are as easy taken as snuff." How so? "You have a fast and prayer day," he bantered, "in which I compute five hundred thousand petitions were offered up to the same effect in New England." Adding to that, every family praying twice a day (through that winter of conflict) totaling "forty-five millions of prayers; which set against the prayers of a few priests in the garrison, to the Virgin Mary," Franklin scoffed, "give a vast balance in your favor."

Slavery was another controversial issue that found its defense in God's will and intervention in answer to prayer. That institution was defended not only by slaveholders but by preachers and theologians as well. According to Timothy Smith, "Princeton professors joined Southern preachers in working out a maddeningly ingenious defense of slavery. . . . God had chosen some to be masters and some to be servants, the argument ran, in much the same way as certain men were elected to be saved and others to be damned." In 1851, Robert Lewis Dabney, a Presbyterian theologian, set forth the proslavery strategy: "Here is our policy, then, to push the Bible argument continually, to drive Abolitionism to the wall, to compel it to assume an anti-Christian position."

God's voice was also what some women claimed spurred them on in the nineteenth-century suffrage and temperance movement. In fact, one of the most notorious leaders of the temperance movement insisted she received her orders directly from God. Carry Nation, known for her hatchet-wielding terrorism, awakened one morning to a "murmuring musical" voice saying, "Go to Kiowa," and "I'll stand by you." What was God telling her to do? To "smash" a saloon. "I threw as hard, and as fast as I could," she later recalled, "smashing mirrors and bottles and glasses and it was astonishing how quickly this was done. These men seemed terrified, threw up their hands and backed up in the corner. My strength was that of a giant. I felt invincible. God was certainly standing by me."

Was it God's voice that Carry Nation heard? Was the voice of God (through Scripture) confirming the institution of slavery? Is God speaking in the public square today through a voice or through biblical affirmation? *Who Speaks for God?* That is the title of a book by Jim Wallis, and it's a thought-provoking question, especially as it relates to public policy.

WHO SPEAKS FOR GOD?

As I'm sitting at my computer writing this chapter, I can hear *CNN Headline News* from the TV in my bedroom across the hall. Chief Justice Ray Moore of the Alabama Supreme Court has refused to remove his 5,300-pound granite monument to the Ten Commandments from the rotunda of the state judicial building in Montgomery. He had installed it surreptitiously two years ago and was ordered by a U.S. district judge to remove it, with the threat of a $5,000 per day fine. It did not help his cause when the eight other judges on the state supreme court concurred with the district judge. In defending his action he declared in Martin Luther fashion, "I cannot forsake my conscience," and further testified: "I will never deny the God upon whom our laws and country depend."

Who speaks for God in the public square? Ray Moore and his supporters would insist that Moore is speaking for God. The *Grand Rapids Press* carried this story (August 22, 2003) with the headline, "Justice: I Shall Not Budge." It included three photos and covered most of the page.

Squeezed alongside was a five-paragraph article with a much smaller headline: "Heat Toll in France May Hit 10,000." Who speaks for God in this instance? Are we to assume God was sending a message through this tragedy, or was God silent? Should someone have emerged to speak for God? President Jacques Chirac, on his summer holiday in Canada, did not even address the situation until he returned home.

"Who *does* speak for God?" asks Jim Wallis. "It's a good question, and a very old one, as kings, presidents, generals, popes, preachers, and prophets of every stripe have enlisted the name of God to bless and support their various causes and schemes." Wallis points out that many individuals involved in good causes have invoked God's name in championing their cause, citing Martin Luther King and Desmond Tutu. But he also notes that leaders of the Ku Klux Klan and David Koresh of the Branch Davidians claimed that God was speaking to them and championing their activities. Is there any criteria for discerning the "voice of God" in the public square? Is God a Republican or Democrat or a member of the Labor or Conservative Party? Wallis wrestles with these issues:

> Is there a reliable guide to when we are really hearing the voice of God, or just a self interested or even quite ungodly voice in the language of heaven? I think there is. Who speaks for God? *When the voice of God is invoked on behalf of those who have no voice, it is time to listen. But when the name of God is used to benefit the interests of those who are speaking, it is time to be very careful. . . .*
>
> Virtually every religiously based social movement of great historical significance has been *on behalf of others.* Slaves, women, children, oppressed peoples, racial minorities, exploited workers, political prisoners, refugees, disenfranchised populations, persecuted believers, and victims of war have all been the subjects of religiously and morally inspired social movements.

The viewpoint of the religious right, as Wallis argues, is generally associated, at least by the media, with the Christian perspective. Jerry Falwell and Pat Robertson are perceived to speak for Christians—and for God—at least in the minds of many of their followers. But Wallis suggests a little exercise to test whether most people truly believe the religious right speaks for God. Go out on a street corner and ask passersby, "What do the words *evangelical Christian* mean to you?" The responses Wallis has gotten are: "Religious Right" or "right-wing" or "Fundamentalist" or "conservative Republican." When he pushes for more specifics, "a whole series of 'antis' is quite predictable: not only 'antiabortion,' but also 'antiliberal,' 'antifeminist,' 'antigay,' 'anti-secular humanist,' 'antiwelfare,' 'anti-affirmative action,' 'antiimmigration,' 'antienvironmentalist,' 'antihomeless.'"

> Let's . . . take another poll on that street corner. Ask those same passersby what they think Jesus was like. Almost universally, whether those being questioned are themselves religious or not, you will hear things like "compassionate," "loving," "caring," "humble," "friend of the poor and outcasts," "forgiving of sinners," "critic of the establishment," "nonviolent peacemaker," "reconciler." . . . How do we explain the contradictions here? Either the popular picture of Jesus is mistaken or Pat Robertson's Christian Coalition has the wrong political agenda.

Who then speaks for God? "God speaks for God," Wallis insists. "And it is the voiceless and the powerless for whom the voice of God has always been authentically raised." But the Wallis *test* is not always clear-cut. One individual, long before Jim Wallis, who was convinced God speaks for the voiceless and powerless was John Brown. He is known in American history for his involvement in the Bleeding Kansas era (particularly his instigation of the Pottawatomie Massacre) and his raid on Harper's Ferry. The son of Connecticut Calvinists, he was a "militant Messianic abolitionist," who inspired the expansion of slave education and the

Underground Railroad. "The Story of John Brown will mean little to those who do not believe that God governs the world," wrote his contemporary Franklin Sanborn, "and that He makes His will known in advance to certain chosen men and women who perform it, consciously or unconsciously." He compared Brown to Oliver Cromwell and showed how Brown's Calvinistic understanding of the Bible guided him.

But Brown did not merely interpret the Scripture, he heard the voice of God commanding him to go into battle. The voice came to Brown in 1855, when he was alone with his wife, but it quickly became the justification for others to act. His account is told by an attorney, Daniel B. Hodley, who did not know the stranger, Brown, who had entered his office:

> Waving a letter received from his beleaguered sons in Kansas, he said that despite his peaceable principles, he intended to go to their defense. At North Elba, with his wife, he turned to the New Testament for guidance. Finding none, he turned to the Old Testament where he read, "And the Lord said to Saul, Go out and slay the Philistines." He and Mary had then knelt in prayer and heard the Lord's voice: "John Brown, go to Kansas and slay the Border Ruffians!"

Hodley was impressed by this stranger, and he agreed to arrange a meeting whereby Brown could plead his case—for "guns and money" to rescue Bleeding Kansas from the enemies of God.

Brown's later raid at Harper's Ferry gave him temporary control of that federal arsenal, but slaves did not come to his aid as he had anticipated. The following day he was overpowered by the U.S. Marines, and he was later hanged for treason. He would become a martyr for the cause of abolition and one of the most controversial figures in American history.

What abolition was for John Brown, anti-abortion was for Paul Hill. John Brown, fifty-eight, husband and father, was hanged on Friday, December 2, 1859. Hill, forty-nine, husband and father, was put to death by lethal injection on September 3, 2003. Unlike Brown, Hill was at one time an ordained minister. Both believed God had called them to violent action on behalf of the voiceless and powerless, and both left behind testimonials. Paul Hill's chilling testimony was posted on the Internet, defending his killing of a doctor who performed abortions and a man who was with him. Hill was convinced he had heard the voice of God, though his story begins many years earlier. He graduated from seminary in 1984 and then served in pastoral ministry in the Presbyterian Church in America and later in the Orthodox Presbyterian Church. He left the ministry after seven years and got involved in what he called "pro-life activism." He describes how the idea came to him to step up his actions.

> Friday, as was my practice, I went to the abortion clinic. . . . I discovered that the abortionist had arrived a few minutes *prior* to the police security guard. This information was like a bright green light, signaling me on.
>
> For months my wife had planned to take our children on a trip to visit my parents, and to take my son to summer camp. . . . I would have the remainder of the day that she left, and all of Thursday, to prepare to act on Friday, just eight days after the idea first struck me. . . . God had opened a window of opportunity. . . .
>
> Saturday, the second day after I began to consider taking action, we went as a family to the beach. . . . All my paternal instincts were stirred as I played with my children. They enjoyed their father's attention. . . . If I had not acted when I did, it would have been a direct and unconscionable sin of disobedience. . . . I was certain, and still am, that God called me to obey His revealed will at that particular time. . . .
>
> In spite of my careful plans, the morning of the shooting was not easy. Although I had gone to bed late, I forced myself to rise about

4 A.M. to spend time in prayer and Bible reading, and to prepare myself for the day. . . . Obedience was the only option.

In an interview shortly before he was executed, Hill suggested that the state of Florida would be making him a martyr, and he hoped that more people, through his example, would kill abortion doctors. "The sooner I am executed . . . the sooner I am going to heaven," he declared. "I expect a great reward in heaven, I am looking forward to glory. I don't feel remorse."

Even the most ardent anti-abortion groups condemned Hill, insisting that God was not on his side. God would never give orders to kill, as Hill had claimed. But who is to be the judge of the legitimate voice of God? Jim Wallis argues that those who speak for God represent the voiceless and the powerless, and the unborn certainly fall into that category, but few would claim that God was speaking to Hill, or that Hill was speaking for God.

If God is speaking today, is it only regarding personal matters, or is God intervening in the marketplace as well? And if so, how? How does God speak today on matters of abortion or on matters relating to terrorism? Was the voice of God's judgment evident in the events of 9/11, as Jerry Falwell and Pat Robertson claimed?

SPIRITUAL WARFARE

Many Christians insist that God speaks in the marketplace today through spiritual warfare. C. Peter Wagner, a professor at Fuller Theological Seminary, has been the preeminent theoretician behind the spiritual warfare movement. In his book *Warfare Prayer,* he writes about "strategic-level spiritual warfare . . . of identifying and binding the territorial spirits controlling cities." The widespread interest in spiritual warfare, according to Wagner, came through a fictional work: "Undoubtedly, the single-most influential event that has stimulated interest in strategic-level spiritual warfare among American Christians was the publication of Frank Peretti's two novels, *This Present Darkness* and *Piercing the Darkness.*"

Through warfare prayer, demonic powers were *evicted* from Adrogue, a suburb of Buenos Aires. "At 11:45 that evening, they [two hundred people praying] collectively felt something break in the spiritual realm. . . . The year of the victory was 1987!" But while the *break* came in the *spiritual realm,* the focus is on down-to-earth politics and economics; political leaders controlled by the adversary are mentioned by name.

Warfare prayer is not for the timid or weak. In a chapter subsection titled "Calling the Generals," Wagner features the work of his wife, Doris, and their friend Cindy Jacobs, an "expert" in warfare prayer from the organization Generals of Intercession. They traveled to Argentina to train teams of people to "engage in frontline warfare." Dozens of the trainees congregated at a crowded plaza and "engaged the spirits in five hours of spiritual battle. Only then did God give them an assurance in their spirits that they had broken through."

Wagner makes several interesting observations about warfare prayer. It is "a new concept to the great majority of American Christians" (and, in fact, to Christians everywhere). "God has gifted, called and anointed certain individuals who were unusually powerful in the ministry of intercession." Closely connected to the ministry of warfare prayer is "another spiritual dimension, . . . personal prophecy." He tells how Dick Mills phoned him with a prophecy that "God was calling me to serve as a catalyst to help" weave together a "three-fold cord. . . . The three cords are the *conservative evangelicals,* the *charismatics* and the *conscientious liberals.*"

As in many instances when people claim God is uniquely speaking or acting, Wagner does not disguise the elitism. Only a few possess such an intimate connection with God. "I myself feel that God may be calling, equipping and enabling a relatively small number of Christian leaders to move out in frontline, strategic-level spiritual warfare," he writes. "God, I think, is in the process of choosing an expanding corps of spiritual

Green Berets . . . who will engage in the crucial high-level battles against the rulers of darkness." What have these spiritual Green Berets accomplished? Among other things, they have been able "to bring down the Berlin Wall and the Iron Curtain" and "to depose Manuel Noriega." They were able "to lower the crime rate in Los Angeles during the 1984 Olympics," and Wagner writes, "I believe God used my wife, Doris, and Cindy Jacobs to turn around the economy in Argentina." Also, "I feel sure the territorial spirits over Japan received a significant setback."

Any turnaround in Argentina's economy was temporary, at best, but even if that nation's economy had made a full recovery, dare anyone make such pronouncements in the name of God? Dare we make the claim that *our* prayer accomplished such a feat?

Who speaks for God? Jim Wallis asks. *God speaks for God.*

The scary thing is that while it is true that God speaks for God, in a real sense we as Christians speak for God. To most people, God is silent. Without knowledge of the Scripture, they have no recognition of God's voice—except for how they may perceive Christians to be echoing that voice. Indeed, Christians are to be "living letters." Essentially that means they are to be the *incarnate* words of God.

I recently read a newspaper article that captured my attention. It was about a court hearing before a judge who was sentencing Paul Samoei, a twenty-two-year-old Kenyan exchange student, for his part in an auto accident that killed two high school boys. Samoei was returning home from his part-time job when he was apparently distracted, crossed the center line and crashed head-on into the other vehicle, killing both boys instantly. The article told how Jill Wegner, the mother of Brett, one of the boys who died, visited Samoei who was in the hospital recovering from injuries. In the midst of her own blinding grief, she somehow thought of the young man responsible for the terrible tragedy. "Tears were rolling down his face," she recalled. "In his room, there was nothing, no support at all. I felt awful." She continued to visit him, and after he was released from the hospital, Brett's siblings often stopped at his apartment to visit him. "Their friendship was most important," Samoei said. "It felt so good, like, I don't know, a feeling I can't express. I try to bring it up to tell you, but it is something really good who they are."

Both mothers asked the judge not to sentence Samoei to prison. The judge sentenced him to one year probation. When questioned about her attitude, Wegner said, "I don't feel it's remarkable that we can forgive."

I searched the article for some reference to Christian faith that motivated these women to respond in such a charitable way, but there was nothing. Perhaps I was not the only one who was looking for a clue that would solve this puzzle. How is it humanly possible for someone in the depths of such sorrow to reach out to the one who was to blame for the suffering? Was it the power of resurrection faith? I don't know. The article didn't say. But it did occur to me that it should not be necessary to identify such an individual as a Christian. The Christian faith should so radiate in the public square that when such a story is told, Christians are immediately *suspect*—whether responsible or not.

The voice of God should be heard in the public square—and it should be so recognizable that it needs neither identification nor interpretation.

2

MIXED MESSAGES

The Varied Voices of God Through the Ages

One can find a practically endless supply of stories about people hearing God, and each is of considerable interest in its own right. I love to dwell on them myself, and I have noticed that other people rarely tire of hearing them, even when they do not entirely believe them."

DALLAS WILLARD, *HEARING GOD*

Some years ago while traveling with Carlton, my then-teenage son, to a family reunion in the Finger Lakes region of New York state, we stopped by a nineteenth-century, white clapboard farmhouse along a country road near Palmyra, New York. It was a historical site that I had wanted to visit, and my son dutifully came along. After a guide showed us through the house, we were directed to a wooded area across the road. We walked down the path until we came to a marker that told of a remarkable event that had occurred some 175 years earlier.

It was in the spring of 1820 that a teenage boy went out into those woods to pray. He had gone for a distinct purpose: "to inquire of the Lord . . . which of all the sects was right." He was troubled, as many people have been before and since, by the growing numbers of churches of different denominations, and his specific question, as the story goes, was: "Which should I join?" The three churches on the main intersection of Palmyra were Methodist, Presbyterian and Baptist, none of which claimed the membership of his family. The Lord answered, as the testimony continues, not by pointing to a particular denomination but rather by telling him that he should join none of them, that "all their creeds were an abomination in his sight." Those words led to the founding of not just another Christian denomination but of a new religious movement, the Mormon Church, which alone claims to have the truth of the "restored gospel"—restored by Joseph Smith Jr., the teenage boy who prayed in the woods. That event, more than any other, marks the origin of the Church of Jesus Christ of Latter-day Saints.

What are we to make of young Joseph Smith and his hearing the voice of God? From the research I have done on his life and heritage, it appears that he, like most adolescents, had absorbed a lot of his parents' opinions, particularly his father's. In fact, the very words that the Lord ("the Personage") allegedly said to the boy had been voiced by his father on many occasions.

As my son and I continued on to visit other Mormon historical sites, I couldn't help but make the comparison between this boy and my own son, wondering if they might have been buddies had Carlton lived in his neighborhood nearly two centuries ago. Perhaps so. As adolescents both had an ability to create mischief, and more. And Carlton, also swayed by the opinions of his parents, was concerned about spiritual matters too. But I cannot envision Carlton going into the woods to pray, expecting God to give him an audible response. I also have serious doubts as to whether young Smith did either. It's worth noting that the account of this visionary voice of God was not recorded until more than a decade later, only after the Mormon Church was founded.

When I hear stories like this, I am sometimes reminded of the story of the farmer who had circular targets high on his barn, and at the center of each one was an arrow. A curious passerby stopped along the road where the farmer was working and asked how he had become such an expert archer. The farmer shrugged and said, "It's easy; I just shoot the arrow at the barn and then go up on my ladder and paint the target around it."

Skeptic that I am, I wonder, when it comes to visions and voices, if the targets are painted around the arrows after the fact. Is it possible (or probable) that Joseph Smith's visionary testimony was created after the church was formed, when it was on the defensive, facing criticism from the outside? Smith, however, was certainly not the first religious leader, nor the last, to claim extrabiblical messages from God.

MODERN PROPHETS

Visions and revelations and voices pose problems for the established church. In the generation in which the Christian faith was born, visionary spirituality was almost commonplace. Indeed, it is hard to imagine Christianity without its miraculous foundations. Paul, converted as a result of the miraculous visionary voice of Jesus, expanded the gospel message—as did Peter, James and John. But with the close of the New Testament era, the boundaries of the new religion became more fixed. There would never be another apostle Paul within Christian orthodoxy. Only outside the perimeters of the church would apostles and prophets with new doctrine appear, invariably authenticated by visions and voices. Within the church there would be countless renewal and reform movements, but such movements, rather than claiming major new doctrines, harked back to the primitive church in an effort to restore pure doctrine or pure living. In most instances, as in the case of the Protestant Reformation, the justification for change was based on Scripture.

The "prophets" that arose through the centuries with new doctrines and new scriptures based their claims on revelations. They are a fascinating assemblage whose stories are as similar as they are different.

Sun Myung Moon was sixteen, two years older than Joseph Smith Jr., when he allegedly experienced an electrifying vision in 1936. It was Easter Sunday. He was praying alone on a mountain in North Korea. Jesus, he later testified, came to him and talked with him, instructing him to finish the mission that Jesus had failed to complete: "The mission for the accomplishment of God's will on earth has been unfulfilled. You, now, must be responsible for the accomplishment of that mission." A dozen years later when Moon was in Pusan, he began dictating to a scribe messages from God that would become *The Divine Principle,* the bible of the Unification Church.

Messages from God that are in the form of an unrecorded voice or conversation are subjective. There is no means of verifying the authenticity of such assertions. But written volumes lend themselves to closer scrutiny. In the case of Ellen G. White, the founder of Seventh-day Adventism, the words have been tested.

As a young woman White began having visions and revelations that in the ensuing years provided unique grounding for the developing Seventh-day Adventist Church, particularly for such pivotal matters as the seventh-day sabbath (Saturday). Her inspired "testimonies," given through a "spirit of prophecy," were both theoretical and practical, many relating to health and interpersonal matters. For example, it was through the spirit of prophecy that she warned: "The marriage covenant covers sins of the darkest hue. . . . Men and women professing godliness debase their own bodies through the indulgence of the corrupt passions and thus lower themselves beneath the brute creation."

Although she claimed that these "testimonies" came directly from God, many of her revelations were later found to be taken directly from published sources. In his book *The White Lie,* Walter Rea, a Seventh-day Adventist minister, alleged that Mrs. White "copied and borrowed almost everything" in her fifty-three books. He offers many examples of direct quotes that she took from other sources without acknowledging them. Her defenders have argued that it was a common practice in the nineteenth century to "borrow" material without acknowledging the source. But in the case of Mrs. White, she did acknowledge a source—that being God—while plagiarizing others.

Even among some of her contemporaries, White's "testimonies" were suspect, and to complicate matters she faced competition. Indeed, there were mixed messages coming from that tiny sect in the late nineteenth century. In 1884, Anna Garmire of Petosky, Michigan, claimed revelations on eschatological events that she prophesied would culminate later that year. Then in 1891, Anna Philips Rice, an evangelist serving in Ogden, Utah, began reporting visions and "testimonies" that attracted the attention of other Adventists, until White quashed them. A few years later Fannie Bolton, White's former assistant, announced that she too was experiencing divine revelations. Without the strong authoritarian leadership of White, the movement might have disintegrated amid the clamoring voices claiming to speak for God.

How do we assess such visions and voices? Are they actually from God? Are they prompted by vivid imaginations or psychological disorders? In the case of Ellen White the voices might have been sparked by dizziness and seizures associated with a childhood head injury, as some have alleged.

In 1975, a century after the heyday of Ellen G. White, Helen Schucman, a New York psychologist and professor of medical psychology at Columbia University, published twelve hundred pages and millions of words from the Lord. She began writing *A Course in Miracles* in the 1960s, after colleagues assured her that the voice she was hearing was not a sign that she was suffering from schizophrenia. The voice, she claimed, was that of Jesus, who dictated the words to her as she wrote them down. "It made no sound," she recounts, "but seemed to be giving me a kind of rapid, inner dictation which I took down in a shorthand notebook." Among other things, Jesus told her that "the Apostles often misunderstood" his teaching, which were then wrongly recorded in the Gospels: "These are some of the examples of upside-down thinking in the New Testament. . . . If the Apostles had not felt guilty, they never could have quoted me as saying, 'I come not to bring peace but a sword.' This is clearly the opposite of everything I taught."

In some respects this three-volume work is similar to Mary Baker Eddy's *Science and Health with Key to the Scriptures*, not only in its content but also in its ponderous style. And like Helen Schucman, Eddy insisted her words were divine revelation: "God has been preparing me during many years for the reception of this final revelation of the absolute divine Principle of scientific mental healing." She "received" the words "by the revelation of Jesus Christ." She "was only a scribe echoing the harmonies of heaven."

Eddy, like Ellen White, was accused of plagiarism, and as with Seventh-day Adventism, there were mixed messages within Christian Science. Others quickly saw an opportunity to offer themselves as a channel through which God could speak. Josephine Woodbury received more than words from God. After she became pregnant, she announced that she had mysteriously undergone a virginal or "immaculate" conception. Some months later she gave birth to a son whom she named "The Prince of Peace." For a time she actually upstaged the flamboyant Mrs. Eddy. Other competitors published magazines and books, but none with the long-standing shelf life of *Science and Health*.

Today God speaks in a language that is more palatable to contemporary spiritual seekers, as demonstrated by Neale Walsch in his bestselling *Conversations with God* and his more recent *The New Revelations*. His is truly a gabby god, with half the three-hundred-plus-page text in bold letters, designating God's words and touting postmodern inclusiveness and self-help. The cover copy portrays him as an ordinary guy:

> Neale Donald Walsch isn't claiming to be the Messiah of a new religion, just a frustrated man who sat down one day with pen in his hand and some tough questions in his heart. As he wrote his questions to God, he realized that God was answering them . . . directly

> . . . through Walsch's pen. The result, far from the apocalyptic predictions or cultic eccentricities you might expect, turns out to be matter-fact, in-your-face wisdom on how to get by in life while remaining true to yourself and your spirituality.

In *The New Revelations,* God promotes the book itself. Walsch informs God: "We need help." God responds (always in bold type): "I know." When Walsch presses God a few lines down about how God is helping, God says, "In many ways." Walsch responds, "Name one." Says God: "This book."

In the first chapter God lays out "Five Steps of Peace" to prevent "the self-destructive direction in which [the world] is moving." The fifth of these steps, like the previous four, is reminiscent of the pop psychology often heard on TV talk shows: "You can choose to live your lives as demonstrations of your highest and grandest beliefs, rather than as denials of them."

Walsch is easily written off as some sort of postmodern, New Age guru spouting religious psychobabble. And Joseph Smith, Sun Myung Moon and Mary Baker Eddy are also viewed as cult leaders outside the range of historic Christian orthodoxy. But many who have claimed messages from God through the centuries were not necessarily regarded as heretical.

MORE PROPHETS

Montanus, a second-century self-appointed prophet in Asia Minor, claimed to be the mouthpiece of the Paraclete—the Holy Spirit. He, along with his attending prophetesses, Maximilla and Pricilla, was, according to Eusebius, "carried away in spirit and wrought up into a certain kind of frenzy and irregular ecstasy, raving, and speaking, and uttering strange things, and proclaiming what was contrary to the institutions that had prevailed in the church."

With the rise of the papacy the voice of God was often associated with that office. The claim that the pope spoke with the infallible authority of the apostles when speaking *ex cathedra* (on faith and morals) did not become part of canon law, however, until Vatican I, in 1870. Critics of the Catholic Church argued that such papal power in actuality stifled the voice of God—especially the voice of God that is associated with mystics and visionaries, of which the Catholic Church has had many.

This struggle between the official authoritative voice of God (represented by the pope and the church hierarchy) on the one hand, and the random and diverse voices of God spoken by mystics, on the other, is portrayed in Fyodor Dostoyevsky's novel *The Brothers Karamozov.* Ivan, an atheist brother, tells a tale of "The Grand Inquisitor." The inquisitor incarcerates the returned Jesus and then reprimands him: "Thou has no right to add anything to what Thou hadst said of old. Why hast Thou come now to hinder us?" Ivan digresses, offering his own opinion that by its very nature the Church cannot permit God to speak or "meddle" now because " 'All has been given by Thee to the Pope,' they say, 'and all, therefore, is still in the Pope's hands, and there is no need for Thee to come now at all.' " Ivan is identifying the age-old struggle between the official *voice* of God in tradition, or Scripture, and the unofficial *voices* of God that come from the mouths of regular folks or mystics, or the returned Messiah himself. Those in power seek to stifle the other voices.

But Ivan's commentary notwithstanding, Catholics have been claiming direct revelation from God since medieval times. Indeed, the Middle Ages were known for spectacular visions and revelations. Bridget of Sweden, for example, confirmed the immaculate conception—that Mary was sinless—through a vision. Catherine of Siena gave the doctrine a new twist by alleging a direct revelation from God that Mary was not perfected until she was three hours old.

These visionaries often claimed specific messages from God about the deceased and their eternal fate. Such revelations were commonplace at the convent at Hefla in Germany, where mysticism thrived. Gertrude the Great and two other nuns, both named Mechtild, were widely recognized for their communications from God. "They provided information about what practices Christ wished performed [for the dead] and about the state of souls in the afterlife," writes Caroline Bynum. They believed that "Christ himself guaranteed the efficacy of their prayers, particularly for removing souls from purgatory." Hildegard of Bingen, another noted mystic, gave vivid descriptions of purgatory—a place filled with "boiling pitch and sulphur" and crawling with "wasps and scorpions" and "sharp-toothed worms."

Roman Catholicism has two distinct, though often overlapping, contemplative traditions. One features a garrulous God of words and revelations; the other values silence. Thomas Merton, a twentieth-century mystic, represents the latter tradition. He was a Trappist monk, secluded at the Abbey of Gethsemani, known for his writings in the area of spiritual formation that are widely read by Catholics and Protestants alike. In his spiritual autobiography, *The Seven Storey Mountain,* he speaks of the silent voice of God, a voice, however, that speaks very much within the context of Catholic spirituality and the adoration of the Virgin Mary. Upon his return to the abbey, before he had made it his home, he wrote:

> And I felt the deep, deep silence of the night, and the peace, and of holiness enfold me like love, like safety. . . . And the silence that enfolded me, spoke to me, and spoke louder and more eloquently than any voice, and in the middle of that quiet, clean-smelling room, with the moon pouring its peacefulness in through the open window, with the warm night air, I realized truly whose house that was, O glorious Mother of God!
>
> How did I ever get back out of there, into the world, after tasting the sweetness and the kindness of the love with which you wel-

come those that come to say in your house, even only for a few days, O holy Queen of Heaven, and Mother of my Christ?

While he was researching a book on Merton, John Leax, a professor at Houghton College, scheduled a retreat at the Abbey of Gethsemani. He wrote a journal during this time, one entry recalling the chill in the air during the 5:30 vespers and his *listening* to the voice of God—God who had already spoken many centuries before.

> Christ is present.
>
> God in Christ has already done everything. I needn't worry about walking with Christ, as if it were something I could do. I need only sit down in His grace, be still, and listen. What will He tell me? The same thing He told Moses: I AM THAT I AM. He will reveal Himself, not things about Himself, and I will never want to move away.

Here is a silent message for all Christians, profound words as old as time, words that reverberate through the ages. There are no words from God that can exceed these words that God gave Moses amid the flames of that burning bush: I AM THAT I AM.

The claim of God speaking is certainly not limited to those who profess the Christian faith. The voice of God gave birth to Islam. Muslims believe that the Qur'an is literally the voice of God because God spoke it in Arabic, and thus the text is not to be translated into other languages. According to Islamic tradition, a voice from heaven spoke to Muhammad in A.D. 610, commanding him: "Recite! Recite! Recite!" The voice was that of the angel Gabriel, but the words were those of God. In the years following, Muhammad received many more such messages, and his followers memorized the words. It was not until after Muhammad died that the messages from God were turned into a written text, the Qur'an.

VOICE OF GOD, VOICE OF SATAN

Does the voice of God compete with the voice of Satan? Many Christians have alluded to such a conflict. Thomas Merton reported hearing mixed messages in his private contemplation, not necessarily the voices of God and Satan but voices that were pulling him in two different directions. After entering the Trappist abbey in Kentucky, leaving his life of writing behind, he sensed the tug of the world in the form of a disembodied writer. Was he being prompted by God or the enemy?

> There was this shadow, this double, this writer who followed me into the cloister.
>
> He is still on my track. He rides on my shoulders, sometimes like the old man of the sea. I cannot lose him. He still wears the name of Thomas Merton. Is it the name of an enemy?
>
> He is supposed to be dead.
>
> But he stands and meets me in the doorway of all my prayers, and follows me into church. He kneels with me behind the pillar, the Judas, and talks to me all the time in my ear. . . .
>
> And the worst of it is, he has my superiors on his side. They won't kick him out. I can't get rid of him.
>
> Maybe in the end he will kill me, he will drink my blood.
>
> Nobody seems to understand that one of us has to die.

This phenomenon of competing voices appears frequently in church history—especially in the testimonials of women, who were often made to question their calling. Was the voice coming from God or from Satan? Jerena Lee, a widely traveled preacher with the African Methodist Episcopal Church, struggled with this conflict. She heard a distinct voice that said, "Go preach the Gospel!" She responded, "No one will believe me." Again, the voice came, "Preach the Gospel: I will put words in your mouth." But almost immediately after that experience, she had second thoughts—prompted by the opposition of men in her denomination—

and feared that it was Satan who had spoken to her.

Another nineteenth-century woman preacher who heard God calling her was Salome Lincoln. In her case, Satan spoke with same intensity that God did. "While the Spirit of God was saying, 'Go, go,' Satan cried out, 'Woman, woman.' " Catherine Booth, the cofounder (with her husband) of the Salvation Army, gave a similar testimony: "It seemed as if a voice said to me, 'Now if you were to go and testify, you know I would bless it to your own soul as well as to the souls of the people.' I gasped and said in my soul, . . . 'I cannot do it,' and then the devil said, 'Besides, you are not prepared to speak. You will look like a fool and have nothing to say.' "

Many who claim to hear the voice of God also recognize the voice of Satan. But these voices can become confused, depending on one's self-image or theoretical presuppositions. An individual who objects to women in ministry might argue that the voice calling a woman to preach is actually the voice of Satan, not the voice of God.

If we are expecting God to speak today, should we also expect to hear the voice of Satan with the same intensity? I am reminded of a conversation I had with Kayla, my granddaughter who was then six. I had told her about some Muslim friends of mine, and we were talking about people who were Christians as opposed to Muslims. She began naming almost everyone she knew, identifying them as Christians. I asked her if she knew anyone who wasn't a Christian. She frowned in disbelief (on hearing such a stupid question) and responded "Satan." She had learned from Grandma Sandy that Satan is the one who tells her to steal candy when her mom isn't watching. When that happens, she is supposed to say, with a forceful gesture, "Get behind me, Satan!" (If Satan ever tries to stifle a call to preach, maybe she will remember the words and the gesture.)

Women who claim the voice of God to authenticate their ministry should not be dismissed. But men have made similar claims. Sometimes the voices and visions and miracles are used to bolster their particular theological persuasion or to show God's blessing on evangelistic outreach—stories that are then passed on and embellished and become evangelical legends. It is an unfortunate but well-known fact that those in ministry often exaggerate their "spiritual victories." I have often heard people purposefully embellish a story or exaggerate the numbers, and then jokingly say, "evangelistically speaking, that is."

One of the legends I heard as a youth related to speaking in tongues. There are two versions: one for God and one for Satan. I grew up in circles that disapproved of the gift of tongues, at least for this dispensation (or age), and we had our stories to prove its pitfalls. One story featured a man who stood up in church and spoke in tongues. A missionary from Thailand (or some other faraway country) just happened to be present. It turns out the individual who was supposed to be praising God in tongues was actually cursing God in the Thai language. Satan was speaking through this individual. But our tongues-speaking counterparts had their own stories, which were better than ours. An American Christian who spoke no Japanese was on a flight to Tokyo, sitting next to a Japanese woman who spoke no English. The Christian presented the gospel through the gift of tongues in flawless Japanese, and the Japanese woman became a Christian. It was God, as the story goes, who was doing the speaking.

We curse and we witness in tongues, and we love the story—if it is the right version.

Another popular story is that of a missionary and his wife in a faraway land having to cross a desert at night to take their sick infant to a doctor. They arrive safely at the doctor's house, and the child's life is spared. Later on, the most infamous bandit in the land is converted, and he tells the missionary how he and his men watched them cross the desert that moonlit night; they planned to attack and kill the couple, and steal their money. But instead, the bandits quickly made their escape when they realized the couple was accompanied by dozens of soldiers. *But we were alone with our baby,* the missionary insists . . .

Mormon missionaries have a very similar version of that story: God's miraculous vision or voice protects those who are faithful.

Citing visions and voices and revelations to confirm belief in the Bible or bolster credibility as a missionary is very subjective. Yet throughout history such has been a common practice. Indeed, many Christian leaders have insisted that without supernatural signs, the Christian faith is weak and ineffective. G. Campbell Morgan was rigid in his assessment, implying that an individual who did not hear the voice of God was a lesser Christian if a Christian at all. And the voice of which he spoke was not necessarily a sweet voice of comfort:

> You have never heard the voice of God, and you say: "The day of miracles is past." . . . Beloved, you are living still among the flesh-pots and garlic of Egypt. You are still in slavery. . . . You know no disturbing voice? . . . My brother, you are living still in the land of slavery, in the land of darkness."

A. W. Tozer, who also testified to hearing God's voice, was far more accepting of those who had no such experiences. In his biographical study of A. B. Simpson, the founder of the Christian and Missionary Alliance, he expressed compassion for Margaret Simpson who heard no voice:

> The wife of a prophet has no easy road to travel. She cannot always see her husband's vision, yet as his wife she must go along with him wherever his vision takes him. . . . From affluence and high social position she is called suddenly to poverty and near-ostracism. . . . Mr. Simpson had heard the Voice ordering him out, and he went without fear. His wife had heard nothing, but she was compelled to go anyway. That she was a bit unsympathetic at times has been held against her by many. That she managed to keep within far sight of her absent-minded high soaring husband should be set down to her everlasting honor.

Hearing the voice of God is not exact science. God—if indeed God is talking—sends mixed messages. And those who *hear* interpret the messages differently. Throughout history, the voice of God has been exploited to bolster the cause of individuals and groups, whether that cause was the Crusades or abolition or anti-abortion or saving souls. Those who would buttress their ambitions by citing God's approval ought to be ever aware of mixed messages that have been ascribed to God throughout the course of history. They would also do well to check their motives before confidently claiming God's sanction for their own agenda.

THE LOVE OF CHRIST

The way to differentiate the voice of God amid mixed messages, many people would argue, is to test the message of the voice by Scripture. So by that means, Joseph Smith Jr. fails while the individual whose message does not violate Scripture passes. But even when we pass on the voice of God, we get mixed messages that are all too often prompted by mixed motives. We do not easily understand our own motives, and this is a factor that should prompt us to remain silent even in instances when we believe we have heard the voice of God. If our silent expression of that voice comes forth in a way that radiates the love of Christ in word and deed, we can conclude that God has truly spoken.

3

KNOWING THE MIND OF GOD

Apologetics with All the Answers

There is greater comfort in the substance of silence than in the answer to a question. . . . The things of time are in connivance with eternity. All things change and die and disappear. Questions arise, assume their actuality, and also disappear. In this hour I shall cease to ask them, and silence shall be my answer.

THOMAS MERTON, "THE FIRE WATCH"

My young adult life was spent mainly in evangelical and fundamentalist circles. We prided ourselves in knowing that we were "ready always to give an answer to every man that asketh you a reason of the hope that is in you with meekness and fear" (1 Peter 3:15 KJV). Our propositions were logical and rational, and we were convinced that we were accurately speaking for God. Though, truth be told, few people ever asked us for the reason for our hope. Nevertheless we were ready, with some degree of meekness and a healthy dose of fear. We were not of the ilk of the Holy Rollers or charismatics or Pentecostals. They were anti-intellectuals who gave Christianity a bad name with their emotionalism and hand-raising and claims for miracles. Though, strangely, they grew in numbers a lot faster than we did.

Today, this *experiential* form of Christianity is widely found in every denomination and is prominent across the landscape of evangelicalism;

it is even found among some fundamentalists. But rational reasoning has not diminished. Indeed, the discipline of apologetics is alive and well. It has come of age in its own right with no need for meekness or humility. Rather, there is often a sense of superiority, particularly when debating with those who deny Christian beliefs. I was reminded of this air of certainty recently when I read an endorsement of a popular apologetics book. It conveyed brash confidence in rational argumentation: "The author marshals the irrefutable depositions of recognized 'expert witnesses' to build his ironclad case for Jesus Christ."

IN DEFENSE OF GOD

The apologists' tools are science, logic and debate, and while they would never claim visions or voices from God to bolster their arguments, they speak *for* God and particularly *in defense of* God. Their influence is widespread and encompasses many who emphasize higher education and the importance of developing a *Christian mind*—a mind that is able to challenge attacks from the outside, whether in science or philosophy or religion. A noble endeavor, indeed. But in many respects it is an endeavor that claims God's voice and God's mind no less than the visionaries do. Of them, Doug Frank writes:

> Among the progenitors of the new evangelicalism there were not only preachers but also scholars, staffing the growing evangelical seminaries and colleges, writing books, publishing in evangelical magazines. . . . Though they called themselves evangelicals, fundamentalist hearts beat in their chests. They, too, were saved. They believed they knew the answer, that their words captured objective truth in a rational form persuasive to any truly inquiring mind. They called this answer a Christian world-view. It reflected the mind of God. They knew they were right about life's most important questions.

The apostle Paul spoke of not being ashamed of the gospel despite the fact that it was foolishness to the intellectuals of his day. But apologists are easily tempted to offer a makeover of the gospel, one that presents the gospel as intellectually respectable. But is such a gospel authentic? For Doug Frank and many others, "objective truth in a rational form" does nothing to enhance the Christian faith, which was founded on the *mystery* of the incarnation that was as much "foolishness" to a first-century world as it is to our world today. In making his point Frank refers to the happy-clappy jingle we sang as kids: "I'm in-right, out-right, up-right, down-right happy all the time" and recasts it with a different slant that fits many of those speaking for God today: "I'm in-right, out-right, up-right, down-right RIGHT all the time."

Christians do God no favor by claiming to have *ironclad* and *airtight* and *irrefutable* evidence for their biblical beliefs. Any pretense of ironclad proof is potentially recipe for disaster. Too many young adults trained with such airtight arguments have gone up against the opposition and come out on the losing side, and in some instances winning the battle but losing the war, as in losing their faith. Yet there often seems to be a overwhelming sense of obligation for smart Christian apologists and philosophers to defend God or speak for God—sometimes in the most obscure, abstract and lofty terminology.

The most spirited debates in the field of apologetics today are being waged on the Internet. One particular site, "Reformed Epistemology and the Rationality of Religious Belief," features some of the arguments of a well-known Reformed philosopher, Alvin Plantinga, who has taught for many years at the University of Notre Dame. One of the notions he proffers is that of *sensus divinatis,* a concept developed centuries ago by John Calvin. This sixth sense, so to speak, is "a special faculty that God gave us whose 'proper function' is to help us form true beliefs about God." While it is true, the argument goes, that this faculty "has been corrupted by sin," *sensus divinatis* "still allows people to come to true beliefs about

God." But does this special faculty necessarily lead us to the God of the Bible? Surely not, say those who would challenge this version of Reformed apologetics. The "Great Pumpkin" objection is a typical response to such reasoning: "Plantinga argues that standard religious belief can be properly basic, but why stop there? Why not say that belief in the Great Pumpkin could also be properly basic? Why not say that more or less any kind of belief could be properly basic?"

Another response to *sensus divinatis* is to call forth *defeaters,* which are opposing beliefs that suggest that belief in God, for example, is untrue. Philip Quinn "offers two defeaters for religious belief: (1) there is horrendous, pointless evil in the world, and (2) a great many thoughtful, informed, rational, intelligent people—including some of the most brilliant people alive—don't believe in God." Now, of course, any good, upstanding Reformed epistemologist must offer a "defeater defeater" to stay in the game. "In the case of the argument from evil," writes the author of one website:

> there is a standard reply: the so-called "free will defense." This reply says that the explanation for the evil in the world is *free will*—a trait so vital and significant to humankind that it is only natural that we have been so endowed by God. Thus, God is not responsible for evil. Sinful human beings are. If this is a good reply to the argument from evil, then the first of Quinn's defeaters has been defeated.

If some people find such discussions little more than "hollow and deceptive philosophy," as Paul describes in Colossians 2:8, they should not be faulted. But some philosophical concepts are helpful. Indeed, it could be argued that Calvin's sense of the divine *(sensus divinatis)* puts an end to rational apologetics and speculative philosophy. We all have (at least most people do) a sense of a divinity larger than ourselves. That is a built-in trait that we carry with us in this modern, technological age. We believe in God whether such belief is warranted or not. And such a perspective *(sensus divinatis)* is not advanced by a defeater-defeater rational response that marshals forth free will.

In down-to-earth terms the freewill response goes something like this: the reason for the child being killed in an auto accident was due to our free will and our fallen natures. It was not God's design but our own sin—drunk driving, bad driving, faulty workmanship or neglected mechanical upkeep—that caused the accident. The explanations are endless. OK, I respond, I will concede human failure in the auto accident. But what about the earthquake that kills ten thousand people? An easy answer: *human failure; the buildings were not up to code.* Well, what about the young mother with a baby on her back on her way to the market, both killed in a rock slide? *Our free will—our fallen natures* is the answer. Well tell that to the grieving relatives, I say.

William Lane Craig, one of the leading evangelical apologists, goes a step further and turns "the problem of evil" on its head in an attempt to make it a proof for God. He writes:

> In fact, far from being a positive argument for atheism, evil itself turns out, I believe, to be a positive argument for theism. For much of the suffering in the world is moral in nature; that is to say, the suffering inflicted by people on their innocent victims is genuinely evil. But then we may argue as follows:
>
> If God does not exist, objective moral values do not exist.
>
> Evil exists.
>
> Therefore, objective moral values exist—namely, some things are evil!
>
> Therefore, God exists.

SPEAKING *FOR* GOD

Does such logic really help the cause of God? These kinds of apologetical easy answers are simply not convincing for those who struggle to believe in God. Theodicy—the matter of how an all-powerful and good God can permit evil—is the knottiest question of inquiring minds. It is in this issue more than any other that apologists cannot resist the temptation to speak for God. But does God need our defense? God gave no answer to Job, that larger-than-life biblical figure. Job's three friends did, but not God. Today, however, thanks to the foundational work of Greek philosophers, Renaissance humanists, Enlightenment rationalists and modernist thinkers, we can now hear the voice of God through our own logic. God now has answers. As in Neale Walsch's *Conversations with God,* we have books that answer for God, minus the claim of some sort of mystical voice, eliminating any mystery altogether. In *When Skeptics Ask,* Norman Geisler and Ronald Brooks answer the big question from God's point of view:

> One of the things that makes men (and angels) morally perfect is freedom. We have a real choice about what we do. God made us that way so that we could be like Him and could love freely. . . . But in making us that way, He also allowed for the possibility of evil. To be free we had to have not only the opportunity to choose good, but also the ability to choose evil. That was the risk God knowingly took. That doesn't make Him responsible for evil. He created the fact of freedom; we perform the acts of freedom. He made evil possible; men made evil actual. Imperfection came through the abuse of our moral perfection as free creatures.

There are many reasons for apologists devising what often seem to be convoluted answers. One is the genuine effort on the part of apologists to stick up for, or defend, God. Like Job's friends, faced with the inexplicable dilemma of a good God allowing terrible things to happen, they speak for God. They do not strictly speak the words of God like their more charismatic counterparts do; rather they speak *for* God.

John Stackhouse addresses this matter of speaking for God with our ironclad reasoning in his book *Humble Apologetics*. He argues that claims for irrefutable proofs can be "offensive and therefore self-defeating." His thesis is: "If we are going to defend and commend our faith, we must do it with a new mode: with a different voice and a different posture. Our apologetics must be humble." He goes on to offer some sound advice: "we must be careful not to claim too much for what we believe. . . . Apologetics should forgo the triumphalist accents that bespeak a certainty of our own theology claims we cannot have." He quotes Dorothy Sayers who purposely avoided being a "Christian apologist" because, among other things, "it fosters an irritable and domineering temper." Stackhouse warns would-be apologists: "we should abandon apologetic presentations that, to borrow from some actual book titles, presume to put things *Beyond Reasonable Doubt,* that tell us to *Be Sure!* or that, perhaps most famously, provide us with *Evidence That Demands a Verdict.*"

In Reformed circles, second only to the *problem of evil* as an apologetical conundrum is the matter of election. Here we not only have an all-powerful and all-good God allowing evil to run rampant, but we have a good God predetermining only a small percentage of people to be saved. How can anyone make rational sense of such a doctrine? One effort to counter the sting of reproach was set forth by Jonathan Edwards and some of his Calvinistic contemporaries. George Marsden sums up his reasoning, in the context of the glorious millennium soon to be ushered in:

> This amazing future had a remarkable theological implication. During the millennium humans would live in harmony with nature as well as with each other. With the resulting combination of "great health and peace." . . . So since the overwhelming majority of all humans that ever lived would live during the millennium and virtually all of those would be redeemed, the percentage of humans damned would be tiny.

As with apologists today, logic and mathematical statistics carry weight, and "if God damned far fewer than one person in a thousand God's overall governance of the universe looked far more benevolent than if only a select few people would be saved." Several years after Edwards published his calculations, his "close ally, Joseph Bellamy, published a sermon including a chart that used the same statistics to show that the ratio of saved to lost would be more than 17,000 to 1."

But arguing for a low percentage of damned (despite Jesus' warning: narrow is the way; wide is the gate that leads to destruction) is a relatively trivial point in the broader apologetical debate. The most foundational issue on which apologists speak for God is the matter of the very being of this divine being, whose existence has been seriously questioned since Friedrich Nietzsche's devastating critique more than a century ago. The foremost *proof* to counteract the challenge is that of *design*. How could the complexities of our universe, including plant and animal and human life, be the products of chance and evolution? Although that question does not answer all the objections to God's existence, it is a valid question. From my perspective it takes more faith to believe in mindless randomness—in unintelligence begetting intelligence—than in God, but I would also be cautious about being too smug in claiming design as an obvious proof for God.

In his book *A Shattered Visage: The Real Face of Atheism,* Ravi Zacharias tells of going to a lecture by the renowned scientist (and atheist) Stephen Hawking, who is wheelchair bound and almost totally incapacitated. Hawking, through a speech synthesizer, delivered a lecture on determinism, "discussing whether we are the random products of chance." Zacharias concludes, "I had to wonder if any person could have left that crowded lecture hall wondering whether this incredible piece of equipment used by Dr. Hawking was designed or had randomly come about!"—his point being that our bodies and brains and the world in general (Hawking's random products of chance) are far more complex than a speech synthesizer. God, Zacharias is arguing, is a far more intelligent designer than the designer of the synthesizer.

So much of our speaking *for* God consists of what we deem logical "slam-dunks," the *Gotcha!* mentality. It is obvious that no one in the room thought the voice synthesizer randomly evolved. But unlike the cosmos—unlike all of creation—the synthesizer had a manufacturer's name on it, and a patent, and perhaps dozens of engineers and technology and language experts all with identifiable names who contributed to its final design. God does not need slam-dunk defense attorneys speaking for an *existence* that cannot be proved. Our belief in God who designed the universe is ultimately a mystery. It is founded on faith, which in itself is a gift from the very One whose existence cannot be proved. It is not based on a label or a trademark or the expertise of a manufacturer's rep.

A SERIOUS HITCH

Not only do apologists speak for God, but they often promote others who are the ultimate expert apologists for God. Among Protestants, there is only one pope of apologetics. And, like so many of my colleagues and friends, I am guilty of throwing his name out when I need some support for a particular metaphysical position that I am touting. If C. S. Lewis said it, it must be true. Indeed, in many circles it seems that the voice of C. S. Lewis is second only to the voice of God.

In *C. S. Lewis's Case for the Christian Faith,* Richard Purtill almost makes Lewis the philosophical spokesman for God (and the judge and arbiter). Perhaps only a cynic would suggest that God's existence might be in jeopardy but for C. S. Lewis. Purtill's first chapters focus on Lewis's case for the existence of God, and in the conclusion he writes: "Well then, would a reasonable person, an impartial judge, be convinced by Lewis's case for the Christian faith? My answer to that is 'yes.' I count myself a reasonable person, an honest judge of the evidence, and I have been convinced by the arguments given by Lewis." Case closed.

Anyone who could be considered a C. S. Lewis scholar, groupie or devotee is familiar with the Anscombe controversy. For the rest of us, the story needs some explanation. In his book *Miracles,* Lewis argued that naturalism—the theory that life evolved apart from divine design—is not consistent with the human capacity for reasoning. Thus, such a philosophical understanding of the cosmos is self-refuting. Many people thought his logic was brilliant, but not everyone.

The year was 1948, a year after *Miracles* appeared. The setting was the Socratic Club in Oxford. The protagonist was a woman, not an atheist but a Christian, Elizabeth Anscombe, a brilliant Catholic philosopher. Lewis was not prepared for the attack, the "severely critical analysis to which she submitted his arguments." With logic and razor-sharp wit, she showed his "proof" to be found wanting. Although Lewis's most loyal followers remained unconvinced by her reasoning, "many who were at the meeting thought that a conclusive blow had been struck against one of the most fundamental arguments. Certainly after it was all over Lewis himself was in very low spirits."

This duel with Anscombe was a personal and professional blow to Lewis, as was apparently evident to his closest students and colleagues. When several of them were with him shortly afterward, one later reflected, "None of us was at first very cheerful. Lewis was obviously deeply disturbed by his encounter last Monday with Miss Anscombe, who had disproved some of the central theory of his philosophy about Christianity." It was also reported that Hugo Dyson, Lewis's colleague and friend, had sympathetically acknowledged the setback and attempted to put it in a positive light: "very well . . . now he had lost everything and had come to the foot of the Cross." In the years that followed, Lewis wrote primarily children's fantasy tales.

That Lewis should be compelled to leave some of his rational arguments behind and come to the foot of the cross in his apologetics should be seen as a positive development, and Lewis and his readers benefited by the debate. Admitting that his argument contained a "really serious hitch" and that chapter three of *Miracles* "ought to be rewritten," Lewis revised the third chapter for the 1960 edition.

But there have been many, including Victor Reppert, who have continued to strongly defend Lewis's original argument. "The argument fascinated me," writes Reppert, "and as a young Christian I never missed a chance to present it in discussions with skeptics." More recently, Reppert wrote his doctoral dissertation on the topic. His reflection on that endeavor is telling: "Even though my committee was solidly opposed to the conclusion of my argument," he confessed, "they nevertheless passed my dissertation."

So the debates continue—and in the same fashion they have gone on for centuries. A smart graduate student passes his exam while convincing no one of his argument. And God has been defended one more time.

For some, defending God is entertainment. Of Greg Boyd, Lee Strobel writes: "For fun, he debates atheists. He grappled with the late Gordon Stein on the topic 'Does God Exist?' He and pastor-turned-skeptic Dan Barker sparred over 'Did Jesus Rise from the Dead?' " This is one game in the arena that the Christians win. The audiences are made up primarily of Christians, and the Christians always pick the winner. When William Lane Craig debated "an atheist selected by the national spokesman for American Atheists, Inc.," he "powerfully built his case for Christianity while simultaneously dismantling the arguments for atheism." Many people "discovered . . . that Christianity can stand up to rational analysis and rugged scrutiny." It comes as no surprise that "in the end it was no contest. . . . An overwhelming 82 percent walked out concluding that the case for Christianity had been the most compelling." So once again God prevailed. William Lane Craig was "in-right, out-right, up-right, down-right RIGHT all the time." The Christians were happy. Their side had won the match, and atheism's arguments had been dismantled.

THE MIND OF GOD

Those who slam-dunk the atheists are not so different than those who hear a voice in their prayer closets every day. God is known and understood, whether through experience or through rational argument. When Christian *minds* are thoroughly blended with brilliant logic and right creeds and confessions, the mixture reflects the *mind* of God. But a critical element is missing. Indeed, is this truly the mind for which we ought to aspire? Or ought our minds be captured by humility and humble apologetics that are consecrated at the foot of the cross? Philippians 2 contains a hymn about Jesus who "did not consider equality with God something to be grasped" (v. 6). "Let this *mind* be in you, which was also in Christ Jesus" (v. 5 KJV, emphasis added). Jesus humbled himself, and so should we. Yet all too often, at least as others perceive us, we are presenting our Christian minds as equal to God's—as though we know, and therefore reflect, the mind of God.

When we cry out in anguish, Why? Why? Why? God is silent. So also is God silent when we ask the impossible philosophical questions of life. Much of life and much of the very gospel we cling to is shrouded in mystery, and our best apologetical response is often a humble silence rather than a calculated defense of what cannot be rationally defended. We need more "poetry in a prose-flattened world." This was a theme of Walter Brueggemann when he delivered the Lyman Beecher Lectures at Yale University in 1989. He described "a world that is organized in settled formulas, so that even pastoral prayers . . . sound like memos." So conscious are we about proclaiming the precise truth of the gospel, he laments, that we have rendered it lifeless: "There is no danger, no energy, no possibility, no opening for newness." This, he argues, is not the true gospel. Rather it is a distortion: "our technical way of thinking reduces mystery to problem, transforms assurance into certitude, quality into quantity, and . . . takes the categories of biblical faith and represents them in manageable shapes."

A dominant theme in Scripture is *faith*, perhaps summed up best in Hebrews 11: "By faith Abraham . . . By faith Isaac . . . By faith . . . By faith . . ." Jesus said to Thomas, who doubted his resurrection, "Because you have seen me, you have believed; blessed are those who have not seen and yet have believed" (John 20:29). We have not seen Jesus nor heard his voice as Thomas and the disciples did. We believe by *faith*. Yet there are those who want to *prove* the authenticity of Christianity either through rational argumentation or by claiming to hear the voice of God. "I remain loyal to His Name," Oswald Chambers confessed, "although every common-sense fact gives the lie to Him, and declares that He has no more power than a morning mist." That is the testimony of true *faith*. And Chambers defined faith in very specific terminology, warning of false faith, that which is dependent on one's experiences and confident in its own certitude: "Be ruthless with yourself if you are given to talking about the experiences you have had. Faith that is sure of itself is not faith. Faith that is sure of God is the only faith there is."

But is this then a capitulation to *fideism*—that naughty word that is often thrown at those of us who are less than confident of our own certitude and who shy away from rational arguments for God?

Richard H. Popkin defines *fideism* as "the view that truth in religion is ultimately based on faith rather than on reasoning or evidence." The arguments related to fideism are too complicated to present here, but like any *ism* there are degrees of error. Extreme fideists insist that faith is contrary to reason, whereas moderate fideists, like St. Augustine and John Calvin, argued that while faith precedes reason, reason often supports faith. Søren Kierkegaard, sometimes characterized as a radical fideist, believed that a "leap of faith" was necessary to assimilate what could be termed the irrationality or self-contradictions found in the biblical narrative.

Fideists argue that while God's ways might be incomprehensible and offensive to human reasoning, such only demonstrates that human reason is part of our fallen human nature. We accept God as God, an act of faith based on divine revelation that does not necessarily require a leap of faith. This is essentially the position that Donald Bloesch suggests in *The Ground of Certainty:* "My position is much closer to fideism than to rationalism," he writes, "in that I see faith as determining reason and not vice verse. . . . I uphold not a mere fideism but a trinitarian fideism, one that has its source not in the leap of faith but in divine revelation."

It is very tempting in this era of the information superhighway to trade in faith for certainty. Scientific studies and statistics and scholarship of all kinds—answers to everything—are but a computer click away. In a time like this, biblical faith seems weak, threadbare and ragged on the edges, downright old-fashioned. How then do we respond? For some, a humanlike, personalized, talking God looms large in the scheme of certainties. But for those who are more sophisticated and intellectually inclined the solution resides in scientific, philosophical and theological proofs. We have built our very own ivory Tower of Babel—all in honor of God who surely must feel more secure now that the evangelical apologists have finally solved the problem of evil and confirmed that pesky old matter of existence.

REASONABLE FAILURES

But are we truly speaking for God in our philosophical arguments? Do the most brilliantly articulated proofs convince unbelievers to put their faith in God? Lee Strobel claims they do. He tells about a crowd of some eight thousand who had come to hear William Lane Craig debate an atheist. "Forty-seven people entered as nonbelievers and exited as Christians." Although such figures might not seem impressive compared to a Billy Graham crusade, they offer evidence for the effectiveness of rational apologetics. But others, as I have found in my study of those who have walked away from faith, are troubled when the rational apologetics they have come to depend on fail.

In his book *Farewell to God,* Charles Templeton, a one-time associate of Billy Graham, tells of his elation in going up against a bright young atheist, proving his case for Christianity: "I'd beaten the captain of the Yale debating team." But the initial exhilaration quickly faded. His stellar apologetics could not hold back the flood of rational doubts and spiritual emptiness: "there was no real choice. I could stay in the ministry and live a lie or I could make the break. My wife and I packed our few possessions in a rental trailer and started on the road back to Toronto where, nineteen years earlier, I had begun."

"How did I come to lose my faith?" asks Sergei Bulgakov. "It occurred when the poetry of my childhood was squeezed out of my life by the prose of seminary education. I realized that I could not be satisfied with the apologetics of the textbooks. Instead of helping me, they further undermined my faith."

The words of C. S. Lewis challenge us in our eager defense of God. In a poem titled "The Apologist's Evening Prayer," Lewis asks God to deliver him from "the victories that I seem to score" and "from cleverness shot forth" in attempting to prove "Thy divinity." The final line is telling: "Take from me all my trumpery lest I die." Who is this God of the chastened apologist? Lewis addressed God as "thou fair Silence."

4

SOLA SCRIPTURA

The Silent Word of God

The Bible stands like a rock undaunted;
Mid the raging storms of time;
Its pages burn with the truth eternal,
And they glow with a light sublime.

The Bible stands though the hills may tumble,
It will firmly stand when the earth shall crumble;
I will plant my feet on its firm foundation,
For the Bible stands.

HALDOR LILLENAS, "THE BIBLE STANDS"

That gospel song "The Bible Stands," sung to a peppy tune, is one we could all sing from memory. For twelve years of my young adult life I was active in Bible churches: the Woodstock Bible Church, the Crown Point Bible Church and the Whitneyville Bible Church—all loosely affiliated with the Independent Fundamentalist Churches of America. We were accused of being fundamentalists and biblical literalists, charges we accepted as a badge of honor. Our stance on the Bible, however, was not particularly unusual. The Bible to us was the Word of God, albeit with *inerrant* as a required adjective. But we basically believed in the authority of Scripture, as have Christians through the ages. Billy Graham's oft-repeated phrase *the Bible says* was ours too. In fact, the focus on the Word has been part of Protestant spirituality for most of five hundred years. We've all memorized Martin Luther's famous lines that he uttered when standing before the emperor in 1521: "My conscience is captive to the Word of God. I cannot and I will not recant anything, for to go against conscience is neither right nor safe. Here I stand. I cannot do otherwise. God help me. Amen." These words set the stage for the Protestant tradition of *sola scriptura.*

LEANING ON THE WORD

The Bible alone is the authority, not popular culture, not the pope, not tradition—though the biblical canon, it must be remembered, is itself a product of early church *tradition.* Indeed, church tradition plays a much greater role in our faith than we are sometimes willing to admit. But this tradition has grown out of a consensus developed over generations. There are, however, may Christians—and not just the so-called liberals—who would qualify the authority of the Bible, and church tradition, by their emphasis on the private experiences of the moment. They insist that God speaks today in many ways—whether through an audible voice or vision or a "word of knowledge" or other forms of supernatural intervention. That this *voice of God* takes precedent over Scripture is rarely, if ever, argued; the very fact that there is an additional voice can serve to weaken the power of the Word.

One of the great thinkers of a previous generation that I look to in coming to terms with *other* voices is the Dutch theologian Herman Bavinck. In his *Reformed Dogmatics,* Bavinck wrote on this topic in reference to Roman Catholics, but he made similar charges against what he believed to be Protestant errors. He was troubled by all the voices claiming to speak for God.

> When two voices are given to speak to the church, one will always speak with the loudest voice, and human nature and church his-

> tory conspire to teach us that it will always be the human voice not the divine voice speaking in the Bible. It is so in much of Protestantism today, indeed. The voice that carries the day is the voice of so-called individual revelations and communications from heaven that a particular Christian or minister has received, or the impression that a believer has about one thing or another. . . . [T]he traditions of men . . . have supplanted the pure Word of God.

To be sure, Bavinck was going against the grain of the spiritual landscape of not only his own day but also past centuries of mystical communication with God, and most certainly this present era of postmodern spirituality. These communications have come as visionary revelations of the afterlife, both heaven and hell; they have come as unique interpretations of Scripture, as warnings of God's judgment, as demonstrations of God's love, and as personal guidance in a wide array of forms. How do we assess these extrabiblical disclosures? If we must test them by Scripture, that test being the standard rule, why not let Scripture stand alone without them?

Dietrich Bonhoeffer, imprisoned for his active role in opposing Hitler, took solace in *listening* to God through the Scripture, and he likened the relationship to God with the relationship to others that comes through listening: "The first service that one owes to others in the fellowship consists in listening to them. Just as love to God begins with listening to His Word, so the beginning of love for the brethren is learning to listen to them. It is God's love for us that He not only gives us His Word but also lends us His ear." God speaks today through the Bible. But do we then conclude that God does not speak audibly, that God speaks through Scripture alone? The closest we come to God speaking today, some theologians maintain, is *speaking* the Word of God in preaching—speaking forth God's Word. But even preaching is not a foolproof means of speaking the words of God. Some of the worst public speaking and some of the worst expositions of the Bible are spoken from the pulpit by ordained ministers. And there certainly are mixed messages that come from the pulpit. Should they all be ascribed to God?

John Calvin, perhaps more than any other prominent preacher and theologian, set forth the concept that preaching is speaking God's Word. T. H. L. Parker summarizes Calvin's position as follows: "Preaching is the Word of God, first, in the sense that it is an exposition and interpretation of the Bible, which is as much the Word of God as if men 'heard the very words pronounced by God himself.' " Many expositions and interpretations, however, are not only substandard in their delivery but do not faithfully represent the text of Scripture. How can they be equated with the very words pronounced by God? Secondly, according to Parker, Calvin maintains that "preaching is the Word of God because the preacher has been sent and commissioned by God as his ambassador, the one who has authority to speak in His name." But are all preachers necessarily sent and commissioned by God? Some have argued, for example, that a woman, a lay preacher or a "liberal" preacher is not commissioned by God. "Thirdly, preaching is the Word of God in the sense that it is Revelation. It is the Word of God when God speaks through the human words, revealing Himself through them and using them as the vehicle of His grace." Parker continues:

> Calvin will very frequently use the most definite language to assert that the preaching of the gospel is the Word of God. It is as if the congregation "heard the very words pronounced by God himself." A man "preaches so that God may speak to us by the mouth of a man." "And what is the mouth of God? It is a declaration that he makes to us of his will, when he speaks to us by his ministers." . . . We must learn to be humble disciples to receive the doctrine of the gospel and to hear the pastors whom he has sent to us, as if Jesus Christ himself spoke to us in person.

Preaching may be about as close as we come today to *hearing* the voice of God. But preachers are as susceptible as anyone else to misrepresentation, false motives and saying more than the text warrants or God sanctions. Preachers would do well to hear the voice of Charles Tindley—a voice that rises out of the grave to challenge them today. Tindley was born in slavery. At the age of seventeen the only word he could read was *cat,* but by the time he retired from the pastorate of a Philadelphia church of several thousand members, he had an eight-thousand volume library and could read Greek and Hebrew. But he was ever a humble man. On one occasion when he was speaking before a large group of ministers, he began by praying: "Father, speak through me as if I were a telephone, and when you are through hang up." That prayer should be the prayer of all ministers who would humbly preach.

"The word of God is quick, and powerful," as I memorized as a child, "and sharper than any two-edged sword" (Hebrews 4:12 KJV). The Word truly is powerful. We need no other *words* than *the* Word of God. In his classic, *Missionary Methods: St. Paul's or Ours?* Roland Allen insists that the gospel without power is no gospel at all. "St. Paul expected his hearers to be moved," he writes. "He so believed in his preaching that he knew that it was 'the power of God unto salvation.' "

There is *power* in preaching the gospel—in preaching the Word of God. I am reminded of the old hymn "My faith has found a resting place, / Not in device or creed." The last verse is powerful:

My heart is leaning on the Word,
The written Word of God,
Salvation by my Savior's name,
Salvation by his blood.

And the refrain:

I need no other argument,
I need no other plea;

It is enough that Jesus died,
And that he died for me.

We need no other proof or arguments. The gospel story—the very *Word* of God—is sufficient.

That sufficiency also offers a sense of security; we are *safe* in the sufficiency of Scripture. We need not be seeking messages apart from Scripture; we need not feel insecure without a message personally directed to our own situation and needs. J. I. Packer's warning is fitting:

> While it is not for us to forbid God to reveal things apart from scripture, or to do anything else (he is God, after all!), we may properly insist that the New Testament discourages Christians from expecting to receive God's words to them by any other channel than that of attentive application to themselves of what is given to us twentieth-century Christians in holy scripture.

Some Christian leaders, however, seem to downplay the Bible as the voice of God, insisting that an additional voice is crucial. Dallas Willard, for example, identifies three false "interpretations of how God speaks to us," all of which are "surely mistaken and certainly . . . very harmful to our efforts to live a life in which God is heard." In addition to the "message-a-minute view" and the "whatever comes view," he identifies the "it's-all-in-the-Bible view." He introduces the latter position with the crisp sentence, "I believe this . . . view is seriously misguided and very harmful." His primary objection to this view is that "many of the specific circumstances of our lives are simply not dealt with in the Bible." So then, what specific circumstances does God single out for extrabiblical revelation? "The Bible," he reminds us, "will not tell which song you are supposed to sing next Sunday or which verse you should take as a text for a talk or a sermon. Yet it is very likely that God's special leading is claimed for nothing more frequently than for the selection of texts and sermon topics."

That the evidence for God's special leading, apart from Scripture, is based on the frequency of claims for it is skewed logic at best. And why, I wonder, is the selection of sermon texts and topics so frequently requested? An appropriate response might be, not *Get a life!* but *Get a lectionary!* Many denominations have guide books for texts and sermons that follow the church year. In my heritage of expository preaching, the minister often preached long series of sermons through an Old Testament prophet or one of Paul's epistles. His (never *her*) texts were frequently planned out months or even years ahead of time. We tended to look down on those preachers who got their messages on the fly—a word from the Lord Saturday night and sometimes Sunday morning—suspecting it might have been an excuse to avoid hard study during the week. That is not to say that there might be a *sense of God's leading* one to choose a different text than one that had previously been planned, though we should say with caution "God told me" to preach this or that.

Dallas Willard's opposition to the "it's-all-in-the-Bible view" is in some ways comparable to what Jack Deere refers to as "Bible deism." In his book *Surprised by the Voice of God,* Deere tells his own story: how a one-time Bible deist began hearing the voice of God. But his story is not merely a personal disclosure. He indicts a movement. "A Bible deist has a lot in common with the natural deist," he writes. "They both worship the wrong thing. The deists of the eighteenth century worshiped human reason. The Bible deists of today worship the Bible. . . . Bible deists preach and teach the Bible rather than Christ. . . . When the principal thing in your life becomes the study of the Bible, you have become a Bible deist."

What kind of people are Bible deists? "By now," writes Deere, "you've probably figured out that Bible deism is not so much a theology as it is a system that caters to a personality type. It's a system that religiously proud, hurt, intellectual people find hard to pass up. It offers justification for our pride without having to repent of it."

Jack Deere's strong stance against what he calls Bible deism and his enthusiastic endorsement of extrabiblical messages is diametrically opposed to J. I. Packer's insistence that Christians should not expect to "receive God's words . . . by any other channel than that of attentive application to . . . holy scripture."

Both sides would argue that their position is supported by Scripture. Dallas Willard and Jack Deere point to biblical examples of God speaking directly to individuals on a variety of subjects. Likewise, those who heartily sing "The Bible stands like a rock undaunted" and assert that the Bible should be heard as the voice of God, not unpredictably, use the Bible to sustain their position. From their perspective the Bible as the voice of God is the very voice that restricts itself to that one voice.

SURPRISING SILENCE

No one would deny that the Bible provides examples of God speaking. That is not the issue. Rather, the debate centers on when and how and why God spoke, and whether that kind of speaking continues on after the completion of the biblical canon. An important issue is whether God spoke to ordinary folks in biblical times on a routine basis.

Only the tiniest portion of Scripture actually claims to be the spoken words of God, so it is difficult to find scriptural precedent for the testimonials of God's routine and personalized speaking to people today. Indeed, the title of Deere's book, *Surprised by the Voice of God,* speaks for many biblical figures: the voice of God in biblical times was not "surprisingly common," as Deere testifies it is for him. Most of the recorded incidents of God's breaking through and speaking relate to singular events in an individual's life or in the collective life of God's people. There is little mention of God speaking on matters of everyday life and no examples of God giving individuals "words of knowledge" (apart from the prophets whose writings form the very texts of Scripture) to a mediator such as Deere, who then transmits the words to the person to whom God will not speak directly.

The bottom line is this: *Does God speak today as in times of old?* Should I expect God to communicate with me—one who holds in her hands the written Word of God—the same way that God communicated with Adam and Eve? Richard Elliot Friedman argues that times have changed, that God's presence and voice fades over the course of history.

> God disappears in the Bible. Both religious and nonreligious readers should find this impressive and intriguing, each for his or her own reasons. Speaking for myself, I find it astounding. The Bible begins, as nearly everybody knows, with a world in which God is actively and visibly involved, but it does not end that way. Gradually through the course of the Hebrew Bible (also known as the Old Testament . . .), the deity appears less and less to humans, speaks less and less.

There are many scholars who would challenge aspects of Friedman's exegesis, interpretations and conclusions, but his overall thesis merits consideration. He points out that at the same time that we see God appearing and speaking less and less in the course of biblical history, we see a progressively independent role for humankind. In the creation account, God is acting alone, without human involvement. And, apart from Adam and Eve's disobedience in eating the forbidden fruit, God is the one who is doing things. "The first two humans, Adam and Eve, take little responsibility for themselves. They do not design or build anything. When they are embarrassed over their nudity, they do not make clothes; they cover themselves with leaves. It is God who makes their first clothing for them" (see Genesis 3:7, 21). By the time of Noah, things are changing. God provides the design and dimension of the ark, but Noah is expected to build it himself. By the time of Abraham, ten generations later, there is an amazing expansion of what appears to be the freedom and independence of the individual.

> Beyond the accounts of divine commands that Abraham carries out, the narrative also includes a variety of stories in which Abra-

> ham acts on his own initiative. He divides land with his nephew Lot; he battles kings; he takes concubines; he argues with his wife Sarah; on two occasions he tells kings that Sarah is his sister out of fear that they will kill him to get his wife; he arranges his son's marriage. . . . Abraham proceeds to pursue a negotiation over how many righteous people in Sodom and Gomorrah would be enough for God to spare the cities from destruction. . . . The substance of the dialogue is nothing less than a human challenge regarding a divine action.

Friedman sums up his conclusions about the historical narratives of the Hebrew Bible, arguing that not only does "relationship between humans and God change through the course of the Bible," but "What I think is extraordinary is the particular course that this change takes, namely toward fewer divine appearances and ultimately none, and toward greater human responsibility." Although at first glance these findings may seem controversial, Friedman suggests that this "is an area where the orthodox or fundamentalist reader and the critical reader can find mutual concern. Though they may see different reasons behind this development and implications of it, they can both appreciate and be struck by the fact of it."

For virtually all Christians, writes Friedman, "the disappearance of God in the Bible" is a "troubling thought." Some people have suggested that God's disappearance or silence is a sign of his anger toward disobedient humans, but Friedman insists otherwise: "It is precisely when humans are closest to God that they rebel most blatantly. The wilderness generation . . . is pictured as the one generation to have constant visible evidence of their God's presence. And they are pictured as the most rebellious generation of all time." Later, as demonstrated during the generations of Ezra, Nehemiah and Esther, where God's presence is not indicated by supernatural events or spoken words, the people "behave pretty well." Nor is God's hiddenness, which is seen in the psalms and other poetic and prophetic writings, necessarily associated specifically with sin and disobedience.

Why is God's silence so prevalent in the Bible? And why do many Christians today hear no more than the silent voice of God? The standard answer is that they are not listening, or they do not know how to listen. In *God Did Not Ordain Silence,* Christopher Christenson argues that God speaks to people when invited to do so: "God is a gentleman," he writes, "and doesn't force Himself into anyone's life uninvited."

Describing God as a "Gentleman" who requires an invitation is a weak effort to ascribe to God status and sophistication that is wholly unnecessary. In Scripture we find God speaking to many people uninvited, and there are scenes in the Psalms and elsewhere when God does not speak even when invited. Christenson concludes his book with a portion of a Psalm 116:

> I love the Lord, because he
> Has heard my voice and my supplications.
> Because he inclined his ear to me,
> Therefore I will call on him as long as I live. . . .
> Praise the Lord!

But that Psalm does not touch on the matter of Christenson's book: that God does not ordain silence. Nowhere in that psalm is God speaking—though God's *presence* is felt. But the psalms also speak of God hiding and turning away.

HOW LONG, O LORD?

There are many occasions in the Bible when hearing the voice of God elicits more negative connotations than positive. Indeed, for all the talk about *learning to listen to God's voice,* and for all the pent-up longing to hear God speak, when it actually happens it is not necessarily the fuzzy, feel-good experience we imagine it to be. It certainly was not for Abraham, who "had his own encounter with that voice in the land of Moriah," writes Barbara Brown Taylor. "He and God had been in conversation for a quarter of a century by then." But these "conversations" had been relatively routine—as conversations with God go. But the words of God in Genesis 22:2 are not recorded as a conversation. There was no interaction. Rather, the words are from God, and what ominous words they were—less than three dozen words in English, ordering Abraham to kill his son and sacrifice him as a burned offering, and for no good reason. If Abraham had just committed the unpardonable sin, it would not justify the command but would at least give it a context. But there is no context—absolutely none. The only transitional sentence is: "Some time later, God tested Abraham" (22:1).

"God was silent as Abraham saddled his donkey," continues Taylor. "God was silent as the small party set out, and silent for the three days it took them to find the place." God remained silent as Abraham did all that was necessary to prepare the altar. "Never in the history of the world, I think, had there been such a silence. Not one word." And then came the voice of an angel, instructing Abraham to stay the execution. "It was the word he had been waiting for. His son was spared. He had passed the test, but Abraham never talked to God again. In the years that were left to him, he spoke *about* God often enough, but he never again spoke *to* God, and God respected the silence. Their conversation was over. Abraham's reward for obeying God's voice was never to have to hear it again."

So what does the Bible actually have to say about *listening* to the voice of God? This is a question that has troubled many Christians through the centuries. For Joyce Huggett, the matter created conflict with her husband, who insisted the Bible alone was sufficient. "Trapped between this teaching, the anxiety of my friends and an irresistible thirst to know more about listening to God," she writes, "there seemed only one way forward. I would have to search the Bible for myself to see whether it describes the kind of listening to God which had struck a chord within my heart." Among the questions she was specifically seeking to answer was: "Does the Bible address itself to the subject of listening to God?" The first passage she focused on was John 10:14-16, where Jesus is speaking of himself as the Good Shepherd. Here she highlights Jesus' *promise* that the sheep "will listen to my voice." From John, she moves to Psalm 23, where the Lord, the Shepherd, "leads me, restores me, is with me."

She cites other passages far too numerous to mention—though most of them relate to God breaking through in a singular moment to announce something spectacular. Regarding the shepherd passages, two important things stand out in my mind. First, the sheep do not have to move into a mode of meditation to *hear* the shepherd's voice. Rather they hear it while they are doing what they do—graze. Second, their *listening* is not a matter of comprehending but simply recognizing the voice and the presence of the master. In her *listening*, Huggett was receiving messages that were uniquely for her. No single sheep has such access to the shepherd. That fact does not disprove her claim to receive messages from God, but the passages surely do not support such claims.

Despite her Bible study and her longing to hear God's voice, Huggett very honestly admitted after an intense period of contemplative prayer that *hearing* the voice of God is more difficult than she first imagined. She concedes that "many mistakes" are made in discerning whether the voice is God's, her own or the devil's. "For the next twelve months I became far more cautious about listening to God," she writes. "I now realize that we can never be one hundred per cent certain that the picture we see or the voice we hear or the prophecy we speak out is winged to us from God."

Huggett's honesty is refreshing. She recognizes that the voice of God is elusive. It certainly was for the Old Testament prophets. Habakkuk presents an answer from God, but only after he has written in the opening lines, "How long, O Lord, must I call for help, but you do not listen?" (Habakkuk 1:2). Jeremiah mirrors this refrain. He can confidently proclaim, "This is what the Lord Almighty says," but he too suffers from God's silence—and God's rejection.

This sense of absence and rejection was addressed in a sermon by Pope John Paul II during the advent season of 2002. Reflecting on Jeremiah's anguish in chapter 14, John Paul offered words of personal application to his audience:

> The second part of the Canticle (cf. vv. 19-21) is no longer an individual lament in the first person singular, but a collective supplication addressed to God: "Why have you struck *us* a blow that cannot be healed?" (v. 19). In fact, in addition to the sword and hunger, there is a greater tragedy, that of the silence of God who no longer reveals himself and seems to have retreated into his heaven, as if disgusted with humanity's actions. The questions addressed to him are therefore tense and explicit in a typically religious sense: "Have you cast off Judah completely?", or "Is Zion loathsome to you?" (v. 19). Now they feel lonely and forsaken, deprived of peace, salvation and hope. The people, left to themselves, feel as if they were isolated and overcome by terror.
>
> Isn't this existential solitude perhaps the profound source of all the dissatisfaction we also perceive in our day? So much insecurity, so many thoughtless reactions originate in our having abandoned God, the rock of our salvation.

Pope John Paul II turns the tables, suggesting we are abandoning God not vice versa. That is true, and so often our abandonment of God is a result of our perception that God has abandoned us. But silence does not equate with abandonment. We are uncomfortable with silence because it too often denotes absence and, worse yet, nonexistence. In our frustration with silence we formulate words and ascribe them to God. Such is rarely a conscious fabrication. But is it possible that an intense desire for a personal message from God turns the desire into the experience itself? Those, like Joyce Huggett, who are longing to hear the voice of God—especially in troubled times—may unconsciously project their own voice as the voice of God.

WHISPERING HOPE

Silence for many people is unbearable. But we must continually remind ourselves that silence does not mean abandonment, nor does silence mean separation. "Even after one has observed the disappearance of God in the Hebrew Bible," writes Friedman, "one is left with the observation that this tapestry of divine-human acquaintance and divine-human balance and divine-human struggle also includes the possibility of a divine-human reunion."

That divine-human reunion is demonstrated most profoundly in the resurrection. The power of the resurrection of Christ assures us that we too will be reunited in the very presence of God one day. But we sometimes ignore the road to the resurrection. This road of our earthly pilgrimage is headed for a reunion that cannot be rushed. We live essentially in the silence of God. But there is, for the Christian, that whispering hope made possible through the death of Christ on the cross—a cross that led to the tomb and three days of what must have seemed like unbearable silence for the Son of Man. "Lo, in the grave he lay, / Jesus my Savior." Yes. But we so quickly come to the chorus and its triumphal refrain: "Up from the grave he arose." We are uncomfortable with the tomb and the silence it represents. Yet our own angst often parallels that of Jesus. The human cry of despair reflects the timeless cry of Jesus that pierced the dissonance in that hour before the grave engulfed him. We share in the suffering of the silence that followed, especially in those moments when we feel most abandoned by God. But for us there is a comforting voice of Jesus who knows our suffering—albeit a voice that is sometimes smothered amidst our pain. This is not a voice per se but a whisper of hope, "breathing a lesson unheard."

I sensed that whisper at the time of my deepest grief—the indescribable anguish I felt when my mother was killed in a car crash. But I found comfort in the old gospel song "Whispering Hope," sung by Norma Zimmer and Jim Roberts. On the morning of the funeral I played the record over and over again on a little phonograph that I dug out of storage at our old farmhouse. In the face of silence—and what appears to be the absence of God—there remains a whispering hope.

Soft as the voice of an angel,
Breathing a lesson unheard,
Hope with a gentle persuasion
Whispers her comforting word. . . .

Whispering hope, oh how welcome thy voice,
Making my heart in its sorrow rejoice.

5

THE "CALL"

A Treasure Hunt for Finding God's Will

God guides us first through his Word, then through our heartfelt desires, then the wise counsel of others, and then our circumstances. At that point we must rely on our own sound judgment. . . . God gave each of us a brain, and he expects us to put it to good use.

BRUCE K. WALTKE, *FINDING THE WILL OF GOD*

If God is silent, how can we possibly know the will of God? Knowing God's will is one of the most often cited reasons for the necessity of listening to and hearing God's voice. The topic of *knowing the will of God* is the theme of many books, articles and conferences—one that was endlessly discussed in my evangelical circles as I was growing up. It is a topic very fitting for youthful North American Christians who have an unlimited smorgasbord of opportunities before them. But the discussion of God's will has arisen only in recent generations. In centuries past the circumstances of where a person lived, what vocation or trade or common labor he or she pursued, and even who to marry was often predetermined. There was rarely any consideration of the different paths in which God might lead. And that is still true in many parts of the world today.

SEEKING ASSURANCE

The concern for one's future, however, is certainly not confined to those who are Christians. A Christian who wonders what God's will is for his or her life is not so different from a non-Christian who wonders what the future will hold: which university to enter, what vocation to enter and whom to marry. Some seek answers in astrology, fortunetelling, tarot cards or some other psychic formula, but whatever the means, the yearning is similar—finding a sense of assurance in the face of an unknown future. The stakes are high. Anyone who could devise a sure-fire method of knowing God's will, or knowing how to proceed as we take that next faltering step into the future, would merit a Nobel Prize.

Some say, however, that there *is* a sure-fire method of knowing God's will. Just listen to the voice of God. In *Hearing God's Voice,* Henry Blackaby and Richard Blackaby cite dozens of people who heard God's voice. John Bunyan, Hudson Taylor, C. H. Spurgeon and others are presented as examples of those who were led directly by God as opposed to "people who make decisions based merely on what seems most advisable to them." The latter, they say, would insist that "God made people in his image, so we must be capable of making good decisions. After all, he gave us our brains." Conversely, the Blackabys argue that "People who make decisions based merely on what seems most advisable to them will inevitably choose something inferior to God's best. . . . The key is not to make decisions that seem the most reasonable to you but to determine which ones align with God's will."

But what *aligns* with God's will? The Blackabys concede that "There always have been and always will be those who justify bizarre actions with the claim they are acting on direct orders from God." An example they offer is John Beukels, a Reformation revolutionary who claimed visions from God, including one that gave God's sanction to polygamy. For contemporary Christians the practice of polygamy certainly rates as a *bizarre* action, but Beukels may have sincerely believed he heard the voice of God and that he was following a pattern set by the biblical patriarchs. But the Blackabys insist that misreading God's will is "not limited to the psychotic religious gurus of the world." They also cite a pastor who "heard" the voice of God telling him to "build a large, expensive new facility." Some church members warned of problems, but the church went ahead with the project. "Of course the problems *did* materialize, just as the wise church members feared." In this case "the chagrined pastor suddenly heard a new word from God advising him to accept the pastorate of another church, leaving a mountain of debt behind him!" The Blackabys refer to this as "spiritual anarchy."

In hindsight it is easy to identify who the wise and the unwise are. But if the project had not gone belly-up, might the accusations have been reversed? And who is to determine what is or is not spiritual anarchy? Is it a matter of outcome alone? Such voices from God are praised if all turns out well. This is, moreover, one of those stories that would certainly have a very different slant if heard from the pastor's perspective. It is subjective, as are all claims to hearing a special message from God.

A project to "build a large, expensive new facility" that did not go belly-up was the Crystal Cathedral. Under the subtitled "A Ten Million Dollar Prayer," Priscilla Brandt writes about that church in her book *Two-Way Prayer.* "Prayer is more powerful than mechanical, electronic or even atomic energy," she writes. "An instance of such prayer power began early one Saturday in February, 1976." It was then that she met for the first time with Robert Schuller. "After four hours of explaining the biblical principles, I told him that Two-way Prayer had to be experienced to be appreciated. . . . The deepest need on his heart at that point was for the seemingly impossible sum of ten million dollars to build a sanctuary to seat more people." For the next several weeks Brandt prayed every morning for the money.

> One morning God said to me, "Perky, I have heard your prayers for the ten million dollars for the new sanctuary. I will provide it, only don't think it will come about because of the multitude of your words!"
>
> I said, "O.K., Lord. You mean I don't have to pray about it anymore?"
>
> "That's right," was the answer. It was one of those times that the Lord told me: "You've prayed long enough!"

In the months that followed, million-dollar gifts were received "as a direct result of Two-way Prayer," and within a short time "God had provided the entire ten million dollars." The Crystal Cathedral has been successful, at least by megachurch standards. But is that the criterion we offer for knowing we are in the will of God?

"Some people are understandably wary of any talk about hearing a direct word from God," write the Blackabys, "because of the rampant, exaggerated abuses of this claim, both now and throughout history." Here they pinpoint the key problem with those who would claim voices and visions for today—the problem of abuse, which for them is easily solved by sorting out those voices and visions that are legitimate with those that are not. But the moment an individual becomes the arbiter of what is *abuse* in claiming God's voice, we are again in a very subjective realm.

Although the Blackabys insist that God's speaking never reveals "a truth about God that he has not expressed through his written Word," God's speaking is necessary in that it "takes the revelation found in his Word and applies it to our lives." So critical is this application that it separates Christians from non-Christians: "In fact, every Christian must know how to recognize God's voice; otherwise, how can we obey him? Apart from God's personal involvement in our lives, our life experience will be no different from that of nonbelievers."

GOD CALLING

Knowing the will of God relates to any circumstance a Christian faces, but it is perhaps most often associated with vocational decisions, especially vocations related to Christian ministry. Here the *will* of God is communicated by the *call* of God. Where would we be in ministry circles today if it were not for the pastoral *call,* the missionary *call* or the *call* to Christian service? But the emphasis on a ministerial call has been controversial in recent years, particularly among some evangelicals who insist that the claim has been misappropriated. Historically, the call was very important for sectarian and fundamentalist groups that did not require seminary training and ministerial credentials. Almost any lay*man* could enter the ministry by claiming a call from God. It is not surprising that women began to testify of being called by God as well. In most instances they were disparaged. Some, however, insisted that nothing prevented God from uniquely singling out a woman for ministry. John Wesley, for example, spoke out in defense of women preachers: "I think the strength of the cause rests there—on your having an *extraordinary* call. So I am persuaded has everyone of our lay preachers."

The call is often cited today by women who are put on the defensive regarding their ministry. Yet Southern Baptists and countless smaller denominations deny the validity of that call to women—except in the case of overseas missions.

For me, the *missionary call* came the summer I was thirteen. I was in a rustic pavilion with scores of other teenagers at a summer Bible camp in northern Wisconsin. The speaker was making an emotional appeal for us to stand to our feet and indicate that we were answering God's call. It was probably the most anxiety-filled experience I ever endured in a religious setting. Time stood still. My body froze. When I did relax my muscles enough to stand, I was hyperventilating and shaking, too numb to cry. By standing I signified that I had answered the call of God—as did dozens of others with, no doubt, far less dread. But for me at least, whether the appeal came from God or a pumped-up camp speaker, the call to missions became a part of my life from that day to this day forward.

I was reminded of my call recently when I read Wendell Berry's best-selling novel *Jayber Crow.* While a student at The Good Shepherd boarding school, fourteen-year-old Jayber got "the call."

> When I was about fourteen . . . I began to suspect that I might be called to preach. . . . What was so frightening to me about this call was that once it came to you, it was final; there was no arguing with it. You fell blind off your horse, and then you did what the call told you to do. I knew too well that when another Jonah refused the call to preach he was permitted to change his mind in the belly of a great fish. . . .
>
> I knew the story of the boy Samuel, how he was called in the night by a voice speaking his name. . . . One night I got out of bed and went to the window. The sky over the treetops was full of stars. Whispering so as not to waken my roommate, I said, "Speak, Lord; for thy servant heareth." . . .
>
> Though I knew that actually I had heard no voice, I could not dismiss the possibility that it had spoken and I had failed to hear it because of some deficiency in me or something wrong that I had done. My fearful uncertainty lasted for months. . . . Finally I reasoned that in dealing with God you had better give Him the benefit of the doubt. I decided that I had better accept the call that had not come, just in case it had come and I had missed it.

The fictional Jayber Crow did not in the end follow through on the call to be a preacher. Instead he became a small-town barber. Others follow through—though often with regret or misgivings. Elisabeth Elliot tells about her missionary work in South America among the Colorado Indians, before she was married. When she and her partner, despite their best efforts, failed to save the life of a dying native man, she was devastated: "If God had spared Maruja's life," she reasoned, "the whole Quinones tribe might have been delivered from spiritual death. In my heart I could not escape the thought that it was God who had failed. Surely He knew how much was at stake. . . . To my inner cries and questionings no answer came. . . . There was nothing but darkness and silence." Later when her language informant was murdered, she questioned her call to missions, praying and "asking for assurance that the call was God's voice and not a figment of my own mind." When she contemplated her own lack of progress in the work, she wondered, "Had I come here, leaving so much behind, on a fool's errand?"

Another missionary who distinctly heard the call of God was Mother Teresa. She left her comfortable position as a geography teacher and went into the streets to minister to the poorest of the poor. It was not because she had such a profound concern or sense of pity for the sick and homeless in Calcutta—a point that is repeatedly emphasized by those who have been closest to her. She was traveling by train to Darjeeling, India, when she "heard the voice of God." When asked how she could hear a voice amid the noise of a rattling train, she responded: "I was sure it was God's voice. I was certain that He was calling me. The message was clear I must leave the convent to help the poor by living among them. This was a command, something to be done, something definite. I knew where I had to be. But I did not know how to get there."

It is well known that Mother Teresa had not felt fulfilled behind the cloistered walls of an elite girls' school. Apart from the "voice of God," she may have heard voices from the past. As a girl she had read with fascination stories of danger and sacrifice and self-denial, stories about "sisters so poor that they lived in thatched huts with wild animals rampaging through the encampments and hardly enough money for food and clothes," and a story about "a Mother Superior [who] was saved by her orphans from a snake poised to bite."

A familiar narrative in the Bible about the call to preach is the story of

Jonah. Every preacher has a sermon on Jonah, and there are many different lessons and perspectives to derive from this little book of the Bible. The most provocative interpretation of that story that I have read comes from an article written by Eugene Peterson, which I regularly assigned as required reading for my seminary students.

The call to Jonah is an instance when the Bible records God speaking: "Go to the great city of Nineveh and preach against it, because its wickedness has come up before me" (Jonah 1:2). The next verse tells us that Jonah took action, but not as the Lord had commanded: "But Jonah ran away from the LORD and headed for Tarshish." Peterson offers his commentary:

> When Jonah received his prophetic call to preach in Nineveh, he headed the other direction to Tarshish. Tarshish is Gibraltar, or Spain, or some place in that general direction—the jumping-off place of the world, the gates of adventure. . . .
>
> Why Tarshish? For one thing, it is a lot more exciting than Nineveh. . . . Going to Nineveh to preach was not a coveted assignment for a Hebrew prophet with good references. . . . We are called by God to a task and provided a vocation. We respond to the divine initiative, but *we* quickly decide our preferred destination. We are going to be pastors, but not in Nineveh for heaven's sake.

Peterson testifies that as a young pastor he "had been inducted into the pastoral career system: get career counseling, work out career patterns, work yourself up the career ladder." His way of thinking is prevalent: "Somehow, without us noticing it, the pastoral vocation was redefined in terms of American careerism. We quit thinking of the parish as a location for spirituality and started thinking of it as an opportunity for advancement—Tarshish, not Nineveh, was the destination."

GODLIKE ATTRIBUTES

Peterson appropriately focuses on motives when we claim to have heard the voice of God or the call of God—or that we know the will of God. Others agree. "There are few things so presumptuous as a pastoral candidate's statement that he believes he is called to a particular church," writes Gordon T. Smith. "He may have peace about being a candidate, but most Protestant churches require that a group, either in the local church or in the denominational administration, decide in the end whether or not a candidate is assigned to a particular congregation."

In reflecting on the pastoral call, Peterson speaks with insight on God's presence and absence, and how that can effect one's attitude and behavior. "Ironies abound in the pastoral vocation," he writes, "Jonah uses the command of the Lord to avoid the presence of the Lord. Lest we miss the irony, the phrase *Tarshish, away from the presence of the* LORD occurs twice in one verse." Then he asks:

> Why would anyone, who has known God's voice flee from his presence? . . .
>
> It happens in ministry. I flee the face of God for a world of religion, where I can manipulate people and acquire godlike attributes to myself. The moment I entertain the possibility of glory for myself, I want to blot out the face of the Lord and seek a place where I can develop my power.
>
> Anyone can be so tempted, but pastors have the temptation compounded because we have a constituency with which to act godlike. Unlike other temptations, this one easily escapes detection, passing itself off as a virtue.

Claiming God as an ally in decision-making, particularly when other people are involved, can be manipulative and tantamount to spiritual abuse when the person claiming God's sanction is in a position of spiritual authority. I recently heard the bearer of bad news introduce his decision with "I've spent a lot of time in prayer about this," thus implying that a judgment that was otherwise unjust was somehow sanctioned by God.

This is a touchy matter. As Christians we claim to have special access to the leading of God, the leading of the Holy Spirit. But do we too easily manipulate that claim of privileged access to our own advantage? Without even thinking, we readily identify a job promotion or a pastoral promotion or a good buy on a brand new SUV or a bigger and better house as *God's blessing*. But how do we know that because something seems to promote our lifestyle or career that it is what God wants? We praise the Lord and thank the Lord and give testimonies of God's goodness to us, but do we ever think that maybe we are thanking and praising the Lord for things that have little to do with God's will for our lives? Too often, when we pray for something—admission into that Ivy League university, for example—and then get what we pray for, we automatically assume the *answer* to prayer is God's blessing or God's will. Prayer and the desire for the will of God are bound up with very subjective feelings and motives. It is presumptuous to assume that our aspirations are necessarily the same as God's.

A biblical example of discerning the will of God is Gideon and his fleece. We all know the story in Judges 6:36-40. Gideon is up against an evil empire, or at least a coalition of enemy forces who have crossed the Jordan River and are ready to attack. "The Spirit of the LORD came upon Gideon," who then summons troops by blowing his trumpet. But before he goes to battle, he wants to know the outcome. Now it would seem that in a time when God was in direct conversation with his people, Gideon might have simply asked God directly whether he would be victorious. In fact, he implies that God has already said he would be, but he is far less than certain about what he might have heard. So he treats God like some sort of mute—like a person in intensive care who is supposed to squeeze our hand once for *yes* and twice for *no*. Gideon gives God the instructions: "I will place a wool fleece on the threshing floor. If there is dew only on the fleece and all the ground is dry, then I will know that you will save Israel by my hand, as you said." The next morning there is dew on the fleece while the ground is dry. But Gideon is still unsure, so he requests God to reverse the order (dry fleece, damp ground), and "that night God did so."

In college we debated endlessly whether or not it was right to "put out a fleece" in order to find the will of God. There are many versions of this fleece technique. The following is a testimonial I found while surfing the Internet. It comes from a man who speaks of God's guidance coming through physical sensations:

> My wife and I hadn't been out together in awhile, so one day we wanted to take our three-year-old to the babysitter and then go see a movie. The Lord doesn't let us see "R" rated movies or even most "PG-13" movies, so I had narrowed down the list of movies to two or three that seemed like possible candidates. I asked the Lord if it was all right for us to see the first movie, and immediately a faint "sick to my stomach" sensation began to rise up within me. I have learned that this is how I experience a "check" in my spirit, so I thanked the Lord for His guidance and said that we would not go to see that movie. Immediately that sensation dissipated. I asked the Lord about another movie, and immediately a "good" sensation, sort of a happy, loving, even "tickly" sensation rose up in the area of my belly, which I have learned is the way that I usually experience the "inner witness." I thanked the Lord, and the sensation immediately dissipated. As you can see from this example, the "check" is like a "no" answer from the Lord, and the "inner witness" is like a "yes" answer from the Lord.

Trouble is, a movie that makes me feel *tickly* might very well make this man *sick to his stomach*—or vice versa.

FINDING GOD'S WILL

The knack for finding the will of God comes with various options. Some rely more on the voice of God or "inner voice" of conscience and others rely on Scripture and common sense. "There is no simple method," writes Gordon Smith, "of finding God's will."

I would question if there is any method of *finding* God's will. Is God's will a commodity that can be found? Or does the will of God unfold as we make right choices or as we redirect and redeem wrong choices? Some people make God's will some *thing* out there that is hidden—something to be searched for and *found* as with clues in a treasure hunt.

Making right choices is not rocket science, nor is it akin to a telepathic séance. It is a routine activity in life that ideally develops in early childhood and matures with solid moral and ethical foundations and with the passing of years. Decision making is not a mysterious enterprise but a learned skill. We learn this skill primarily through experience, and it is something we do all of the time whether we are skilled or not. And because it is such a routine activity of life, we often fail to contemplate the consequences, unless the stakes are obviously high. But often it is life's little choices that turn us on a different course and have consequences for all eternity.

Gordon Smith identifies two distinct perspectives on what he refers to as divine guidance. There may be more, but his categories are useful in distinguishing two opposing positions: the "blueprint school" and the "wisdom school." The blueprint concept is the belief that "there is one and only one perfect plan for each individual and that this perfect will can be discovered by an examination of signs, or what are often called 'open doors.' " Smith is critical of this school because "it seemingly undercuts . . . the presence and voice of God. . . . Most of all we need to listen to God."

Smith identifies the "wisdom school" most specifically with Garry Friesen and his book *Decision Making and the Will of God*. Friesen argues that "God does not expect his people to look at signs and open doors, or even listen to little voices in their heads," writes Smith. "Rather he believes that through Scripture the Christian's mind is renewed" and we "become increasingly capable of making good choices."

Smith criticizes both schools of thought, asserting that "in both cases God is distant from the decision-making process." In decision making, we "must listen to God. God is present; God does speak; and we can, if we will, hear and respond to his prompting." For support, he cites incidences in the lives of the apostles, particularly in the book of Acts, which "gives testimony to a remarkable sensitivity to the voice of God directing, guiding and prompting"—though he makes no reference to sharp disagreements and apparent wrong choices that Peter and Paul and others made.

But while insisting that *listening to God* is what is missing in discerning the will of God, Smith qualifies his thesis every step of the way, seeming to suggest that we should listen to God but be very cautious in claiming frequent or specific directives:

> Some people have made exaggerated claims regarding God's guidance. They trivialize the guidance of God by claiming that God has provided them with specific directives regarding innumerable situations. They speak constantly of the Lord telling them this or that. We weary of this and may be tempted to react with skepticism. But the abuse of this tremendous gift from God—the voice or prompting of the Spirit—cannot lead us to abandon this provision.

Smith's own model for discerning the will of God is based on "the principle of *friendship with God.*" This involves the "meeting of two wills, both free." But again he qualifies: "We dare not overstate the nature of that friendship or how specific the guidance of God has been. We cannot abuse the gift of God's presence and voice." Unlike many of those who emphasize the "voice" of God, he recognizes the perils of unleashing that voice, making his position appear inconsistent and contradictory: "We need to learn how to listen. . . . God is eager to respond to and guide his children. He is Father and Shepherd and loving King. . . . God does not have a mouth; he does not speak audibly. Rather, God 'speaks' to us through our feelings, impressions left on our minds. But we must not equate the voice in our head with the voice of God."

Smith counsels the reader to "at the very least" set aside a day at "a place of retreat" for "prayer and reflection when you face a critical decision." The person should be alone—not where one is "expected to converse with others or respond to their concerns." But he recognizes that even in a setting such as this, one is not free from sinful and selfish motives.

Such concerns are not Smith's alone. They come from Scripture and from voices through the centuries. John Calvin warned his followers about placing too much stock in the inner witness of the Spirit or individual spiritual illumination. Human beings corrupted by their fallen natures are always susceptible to self-deceit. John Wesley also warned of this self-deceit: "How many have mistaken the voice of their own imagination for the witness of the Spirit of God, and then idly presumed they were the children of God while they were doing the works of the devil."

Garry Friesen no doubt has written the most thought-provoking and controversial book in recent decades on the topic of the will of God. He argues for what he terms the "wisdom view." He concedes that "One apparent strength of the traditional view is the sense that God's leading is personal and direct. . . . The most common misconception of the way of wisdom is that it is impersonal—that God is excluded from the decision-making process."

Friesen cites the apostles, who "never defended their decisions on the basis of inward impulses, which led them to God's 'perfect will.' " He points to a progressive trend in the Bible away from a "leading" involved in decision-making. Such leadings occurred much less in the New Testament than in the Hebrew Bible. Today we look to Scripture, not the inner voice, for guidance, a position supported by Scripture itself. Friesen cites two particular passages: "For everything that was written in the past, was written to teach us, so that through endurance and the encouragement of the Scriptures we might have hope" (Romans 15:4). Likewise, Paul writes to Timothy: "All Scripture is God-breathed and is useful for teaching, rebuking, correcting and training in righteousness, so that the man of God may be thoroughly equipped for every good work" (2 Timothy 3:16-17).

Friesen concedes that his approach to guidance may seem distant and impersonal, but at the same time he warns of the pitfalls of other approaches—especially those that confuse the "still, small voice" of God with an individual's own emotional "voice." He counsels, "One's own feelings are not an authoritative source of direction for making decisions. But because they are mistakenly taken as divine guidance, they are often regarded as being authoritative."

NO VISIONS, NO VOICES

Discerning God's will is not a topic to which we can easily come to a resolution. Gordon Smith, by adding all of his qualifications, illustrates this very clearly, which in the end is less a criticism of him than recognition of the complexity of the matter.

Making decisions is not simplified for someone who does not believe in God or subscribe to biblical principles, as was demonstrated by Jean Paul Sartre, the noted French existentialist and agnostic. The freedom to make choices apart from any consideration of God was an albatross around his neck. "Man is condemned to be free," he lamented. "Condemned because he did not create himself, yet is nevertheless at liberty, and from the moment that he is thrown into this world he is responsible for everything he does. . . . Man is nothing else but . . . the sum of his actions."

Sartre was wrong, and not just from a Christian perspective. Much of what transpires in our lives comes from outside of our choices, events that occur apart from our free will. Whether we see God's hand in our lives or the hand of mindless fate and determinism, our lives belong not solely to ourselves. For the Christian, making right choices and living a life pleasing to God is paramount, but always with the acknowledgment of God's sovereign grace at work entirely apart from our making decisions.

Our lives are tapestries that are woven through the work of God's hands and our own. If we know God's Word and if we "know Christ and the power of his resurrection and the fellowship of sharing in his sufferings" (Philippians 3:10), it is not necessary to receive special messages to *know* the will of God or *do* the will of God. When a person's faith is mature, making decisions and responding to situations come naturally. In *The Transforming Friendship,* Leslie Weatherhead offers an illustration that in many ways should parallel our relationship with God. He introduces the illustration with a question:

> If my friend's mother in a distant town falls ill and he urgently desires to visit her, which would reveal deeper friendship—my lending him my motor-bike in response to his request for it, or my taking it to his door for him as soon as I heard of the need, without waiting to be asked? In the first case there has to be a request made with a voice. But in the second the fact of the friendship creates in me a longing to help. The first illustrates the communication between two persons on what we might call the level of the seen; but the second illustrates the communion, at a deeper level, of two persons on what we may call the level of the unseen.

When our motives and patterns of conduct are attuned to the teaching of Scripture, we act unconsciously in our relationship toward God, others and ourselves. Such actions fulfill the will of God. We need no visions or voices.

If I can't *find* the will of God, how then do I *know* the will of God? I'm often asked this question in one form or another. Here is my personal response: During our first year of marriage, John and I lived together in both of our homes. I had lived in a house for more than a quarter of a century and was hesitant to move from the neighborhood where my son had grown to manhood and where I had bonded with folks as I gardened and walked the dog.

John enjoyed his condo where downtown culture and dining were a leisure walk away—a place that held dear memories of Ruth and Myra and where he had kept a deathwatch twice over as he mourned his widowhood. So we each retained our separate dwellings, dividing our time between two homes ten minutes apart.

We never talked specifically about the *will of God* for our housing. But we did talk a lot about lifestyle issues and consumer culture that bids us buy bigger vehicles and build bigger homes. We are challenged by the simple lifestyle of Mennonite families in comparison to our upwardly mobile friends. At the same time we were almost oblivious to our own affluent lifestyle, sporting not one but two nice homes, with dreams of purchasing an RV. In hindsight we realize how easy it is to censure others as Jesus warned: seeing the sliver in someone else's eye while overlooking the plank in our own.

Then recently while driving through a neighborhood along the Grand River, we noticed a house for sale. It turned out the home had been taken off the market, but the realtor sent us other listings on the river—some priced in the hundreds of thousands, beautiful homes with all the amenities. If we sold both dwellings and got a mortgage, we could afford such a home. But as we talked, the conversations of previous months convicted us. Is this how we should live? What message would this send to our children? To my seminary students? To friends at church? They would not censure us for having a fine home. But is this the best way to be good stewards of our wealth?

One particular house on the river caught our attention. The price was less than a third the cost of our combined homes. We asked to see it and made an offer. John, retired professor-turned-carpenter, saw great possibilities. This house is now ours, and both of our homes are on the market. We have taken an important step in *downward* mobility and that step has led to other lifestyle choices (ones that do not include an RV). Here in this neighborhood of "river rats" we envision opportunities to reach out in friendship to neighbors while strengthening bonds with children and grandchildren who love the riverside setting. We are now planning to use this savings as well as money in other funds to serve others rather than boosting our own lifestyle or that of our heirs.

How do we discover the will of God? We didn't wait for a personalized message from God. John's most oft-quoted verse applied: "Pure religion . . . undefiled before God . . . is this: to visit the fatherless and widows in their affliction and to keep oneself unspotted from the world" (James 1:27 KJV).

6

THE RULES OF LISTENING

Twelve Steps to Hearing God's Voice

James Houck . . . is the last living link to the spiritual roots of the Twelve Step Movement. Since 1996 [he has] taken thousands of people . . . from the bondage of addiction and self-destructive behavior by establishing and maintaining a two-way communication with the "God who speaks."

WALLY PATON, *HOW TO LISTEN TO GOD*

I once lightheartedly suggested to a friend that we coauthor a book—maybe even a bestseller—titled *Twelve Steps to Everything*. The twelve-step movement has gained popularity in recent decades, and it would not be difficult to imagine a "Twelve-Steps to Listening to God" program. *Listening* comes naturally to some people, but for most of us it must be developed. For the individual who takes this matter seriously, training is readily available. These days there is a wide array of books and seminars and websites devoted to *listening skills* and the *art of listening*. The common theme is that relationships improve, sales figures swell and conflicts are diffused when listening skills are employed. It should not surprise us then that some say developing the skill and expertise of listening to God provides similar benefits.

GOD'S VOICE

But does listening to God involve the same set of skills that are needed for listening to friends, coworkers, a stranger or spouse? What is meant by *listening* to God—to *hearing God's voice?* How does someone actually listen to the voice of God? There are many approaches. One is a way of living, a lifestyle of devotion and separation from the world. It is a radical spiritual pilgrimage of mystics and monastics. Silence is valued, and listening to God is a natural aspect of prayer and meditation. This approach has been particularly evident in Catholic circles since the Middle Ages. But is there a biblical precedent for this monastic lifestyle of silence and listening, a spiritual pilgrimage that is often associated with visions and revelations?

God's voice was heard by saints and sinners alike in the Hebrew Bible, without the aid of the cloistered cell. In the New Testament John the Baptist went into the wilderness and Anna and Simeon devoted themselves to temple ministry, but ought they be regarded as models for Christian discipleship? Moreover, we need to keep in mind that the voice of God they heard did not convey personal advice or counsel. Rather, it carried singular prophetic announcements.

For Protestants a celibate way of life separated from the world has never caught on, and in recent years, with the scandal associated with the priesthood, Catholics too are questioning its efficacy. Martin Luther condemned the monastic lifestyle and particularly celibacy, once sarcastically quipping that the monastic concept arose from none other than "the devil in hell and his mother." The Reformers insisted that the Bible, long reserved for Catholic clerics alone, must become our source for communion with God. But the Bible too easily became a textbook to exegete and outline and critique. In the generations that followed the Reformation, pietistic movements and evangelical revivals served as an antidote. The emphasis was on inner spirituality and a personal relationship with Jesus, a religious approach captured in nineteenth- and twentieth-century hymns. This relationship was for all Christians. "I come to the garden alone," we plaintively sang. "And the voice I hear falling on my ear / the Son of God discloses"—the very Son of God who "walks with me, and He talks with me, / And He tells me I am His own."

Protestants, like Catholics, have not been averse to a mystical relationship with God. But in more recent times this relationship has been drained of its mystery and arranged in tidy twelve-step approaches. The style depicts God talking in everyday conversation as with a friend. No cloistered convent is necessary or even desirable. The Bible is often referenced for support. If God conversed with Adam or Noah or Abraham, so the reasoning goes, God converses in the same way with Christians today. That the biblical record of God's speaking involved key individuals and related to consequential matters is typically ignored. Indeed, there is no record of unnamed individuals among the children of Israel, for example, who conversed personally with God.

This conversational approach to communing with God is one that is particularly suited to a contemporary cultural mindset ruled by schedules and lists and appointments. God, just like clients and consultants, is crammed into the calendar. A *quiet time* is taken on the fly—fifteen minutes slotted in before shutting out the light. And to listen to God, one follows a proscribed set of steps.

An important aspect of following these rules is learning how to recognize the voice of God, a mystical concept that is presented in practical terminology. But does God even have a voice? Is such terminology even appropriate when speaking of God?

The recognition of human voices comes through familiarity. A mother's voice is quickly recognized by her infant, and soon other voices are added to the brain's index. An interesting little exercise is to try to tally how many voices you recognize. Most of my friends and relatives do not identify themselves on the phone. They don't have to. I know them well enough to recognize their voices. Is God's voice recognized in a similar way? Do those who recognize the voice of God demonstrate a more intimate familiarity with God? Or does this bring God down to our level? Does this humanize God?

Many who offer advice on this subject emphasize the necessity of *learning* to recognize God's voice by following a set procedure for listening. *Hearing God's Voice* by Henry Blackaby and Richard Blackaby is a typical example of this. "We contend that God *does* speak to people," they write. "However, people must be prepared to hear what he is saying. It is crucial that Christians clearly understand what God is communicating to them." So, *preparation* is a prerequisite, but precisely what preparation is necessary they do not specify. They do, however, cite a missionary to India, John Hyde, known as "Praying Hyde" who "mastered the language of heaven," a language they do not identify.

But "what if there is silence when I pray?" they ask. "What should I do?" They offer three suggestions:

> First, it may be that God is speaking but you have failed to recognize his voice. . . . Make certain that you know God well enough that you can recognize his voice when he speaks. . . .
>
> Second, examine your heart for sin. . . . Silence is a powerful method by which God may be alerting you to sin in your life. . . .
>
> Finally . . . wait upon God in the midst of silence. The Lord may simply want you to trust him and to wait until he reveals something greater to you than you have known before.

Regarding the first response to God's silence, the Blackabys offer five steps to "learning to recognize God's voice"—none of which follow a pattern that was followed by biblical figures. Indeed, it is hard to imagine Adam, Noah, Abraham, Moses or Paul utilizing such a five-step program.

- Develop your relationship.
- Seek to understand God's ways.
- Prepare your heart.

- Learn to concentrate.
- Develop habitual obedience.

In reference to the second response to God's silence, "examining your heart for sin," the Blackabys seem to suggest that God's silence is a form of the *silent treatment*—a silence of anger or at least provocation: "God's silence sends a strong message: we should examine our lives to ensure no sin is provoking him to remain silent."

There is simply no warrant in Scripture to make such a strong claim. Rather, the record shows that God's judgment was most commonly manifested in speech or action, and that it was directed at the nation or the whole people. We are seriously misguided when we speculate about God's apparent silence in matters of right and wrong, and sin in general. The Bible sets forth a strict standard on such matters—one that is too easily ignored when we are trying to read the mind of God in some other fashion. God speaks on sin, and our means of hearing that message is straightforward. I memorized it as a child: "Thy Word have I hid in my heart, that I might not sin against Thee" (Psalm 119:11 KJV).

Regarding the Blackabys' third response—waiting until God "reveals something greater to you than you have known before"—it is another example of privatizing the faith. It fosters a false assumption that God can be manipulated if we hold him hostage to our waiting. Should we really assume our actions, whether waiting or not waiting, will cause God to break the silence and speak?

An overview of the literature of listening reveals many common features, particularly the tendency to speak in vague abstractions and to support viewpoints with personal testimonies. I was surprised, however, to find so much of it written in a linear mode of steps and rules and principles—perhaps a more masculine style of writing than narrative. (Most of the books are, in fact, written by men.) I had not expected a topic as subjective as hearing the voice of God to be garnished with lists, but such is the case. Although the Bible never suggests such steps, the most widely publicized books on the subject do. But personal anecdotes are also included, though in many cases they have a masculine ring to them, as is true of a story told by Jack Deere. It is about hearing the voice of God, but the subject God is dealing with is pornography.

Deere taught at Dallas Theological Seminary for many years—a school known for dispensational fundamentalism. In his recent book, *Surprised by the Voice of God,* Deere describes the atmosphere in that institution: "In my circles, in those days, visions weren't exactly vogue. In fact, having a vision could have been grounds for dismissal, or at least a trip to the faculty psychiatrist's office. As these cold realities began to settle on me, my enthusiasm for my newly found 'word of knowledge' ministry began to sputter."

The opening illustration of the book gives us an example of what he means by his "word of knowledge" ministry. Robert, a student, had stopped by his office to ask for an extension on an assignment. "That's when it happened," Deere explains:

> As I was listening to Robert, he faded away and in his place I *saw* the word "PORNOGRAPHY" in large, capital block letters. . . . For months, I had been praying for God to speak to me like this. . . . I decided not to say anything. Yet, I had been praying for months for God to speak to me like this. A harsh legalistic thought entered my mind. *If this is God speaking to me and I don't say anything to Robert, God may never speak to me like this again.* . . . I decided to obey God.

When Robert denied that he had been struggling with anything that would offend God, Deere decided not to pursue the matter. But, he says, "as soon as I made the decision not to say any more to Robert, the vision came back. This time the word 'pornography' started blinking on and off." After asking again in nonspecific terms, Deere asked point blank, "Are you into pornography?" After he promised to keep the matter confidential, Robert confessed that he was.

The use of the word *surprised* in the title of his book does not fit the description of Deere's experience, which had come after months of prayer. And since then the voice "is surprisingly common," he writes. "What is more, I have come to expect that voice to speak to me, especially when I am attempting to minister to someone in Jesus' name." Deere offers his three steps or prerequisites for God to speak to him "regularly and sometimes in amazing ways"—though he does not list them by number:

if I expect his voice,
if I really *need* his voice, and
if I am diligent in learning how to recognize his voice.

Although Deere laments that "so many of us have been conditioned to read the Bible in terms of *our experience* rather than in terms of the experience of the people in the Bible" (and thus do not believe in and perform modern-day miracles), his own examples look far more like *his* experience than the experience of people in the Bible. As I contemplate Deere's story of Robert and the prerequisites for God speaking, I cannot identify one biblical illustration that would parallel his. In 2 Samuel 2:1 we read that the Lord sent the prophet Nathan to David. Nathan told a parable that caused David to confess his sin—his adultery with Bathsheba, his ordering the death of her husband, and his taking her as his wife. But Nathan approached David after these incidents had become known, after David "had her brought to his house, and she became his wife and bore him a son" (2 Samuel 11:27). There is no record of Nathan hearing this information supernaturally, much less in large block letters. And nowhere is it suggested that others should follow steps or meet prerequisites to emulate Nathan.

Deere's second illustration is about Rhonda, a young woman brought to him because she was having nightmares. "As I began to pray, the name

'Don' kept coming to mind," he writes. "I stopped praying and asked, 'Does the name Don mean anything to you?' Her faced lost its color and seemed to retreat behind a veil of shame." The upshot of the story is that three months earlier she had had an illicit relationship with Don.

That illustration reminded me of an experience I had several years ago. I was doing research on cults and the New Age Movement for a book I was writing, and I attended a meeting one evening at a small spiritualist church in Grand Rapids. The guest speakers were mediums who one at a time stood on the platform and did "readings" on people in the audience (people who stood to indicate a need without identifying themselves or their problems). Most of the mediums were safe. After going into a momentary trancelike meditation, they typically said something like, "I'm seeing the death of someone you loved very much," and from there they led the person on in an interactive and *safe* "reading" of a rather generalized problem or issue.

But there was one woman who had more courage than the rest. She specialized in names. When her first subject rose to his feet, she closed her eyes in a manner of meditation and then asked if a particular name meant anything to him. I don't remember the name, but after a pause the man hesitantly said it did, and he dredged up someone from his past. With that she was on a roll, and after a few minutes of interaction, she was able to relate that particular individual to the man's current situation. The audience, my thirteen-year-old son included, seemed genuinely impressed. This was followed by two or three similar readings. Then a woman seated near the front stood up. After some moments of meditation, the name the medium revealed to the woman was Diane. Now, who among us—baby boomers and older—doesn't have a Diane somewhere in our past? But this woman apparently did not, and no amount of prodding could get her to admit otherwise. The woman on the platform then gave some other names like Doreen and Darlene, but the woman in the audience shook her head each time. It was embarrassing. I actually found myself getting fidgety. It ended when the medium on the platform confessed that she was getting "bad vibrations" from someone in the audience. At that point my son elbowed me—though, to this day I deny any responsibility. That Jack Deere's *Don* was a match and this woman's *Diane* was not is inconclusive proof for God's voice. Psychics too have their Dons.

METHODS OF LISTENING TO GOD

The practice and the prescribed methods of listening to God are reminiscent not only of psychic spirituality but also of non-Christian religions. Some of the practical advice offered by Christians is very similar to that given by those promoting Eastern meditation. In *A Method for Contemplative Prayer,* for example, James Borst suggests several methods to follow for listening to God.

> Just sit down and relax. Slowly and deliberately let all tension flow away, and gently seek an awareness of the immediate and personal presence of God. . . . You can relax and let go of everything, precisely *because* God is present. In his presence nothing really matters; all things are in his hands. Tension, anxiety, worry, frustration all melt away before him, as snow before the sun.
>
> Seek peace and inner silence. Let your mind, heart, and will and feelings become tranquil and serene. Let inner storms subside: obsessional thoughts, passionate desires of will and emotion. "Seek peace and follow after it" (Ps. 34:14).

Joyce Huggett carries the relaxation techniques a step further. In *Listening to God,* she writes, "If I was still conscious of tension, I would tighten every muscle in my body quite deliberately. Then, starting with the facial muscles, I would relax them. At the same time, I would ask God to spread his life and his energy through me. And almost always I became aware that I was being impregnated by God's peace." It was "in this way," she continues, that "I began to serve my apprenticeship in the art of listening to God." She later became part of a gathering that had the same goal in mind.

> For an hour a week, a group of us explored together the basics of listening to God. Together we experimented with various ways of entering into stillness. . . . We tried a number of bodily postures, had fun in discovering together that deep, rhythmical breathing acts as a kind of metronome in prayer, spent time writing in our prayer journals, and learned to meditate in the way I have described in this book: on creation and on God's Word.

When I read her technique of tightening every muscle in her body and then starting a process that began with the face and letting God spread his energy through her whole body, I was reminded of Myrtle Fillmore, the cofounder, with her husband, Charles, of the Unity School of Christianity. Begun in the late nineteenth century, Unity was part of the New Thought movement (similar to Christian Science) and today has opened its doors to all things New Age. Myrtle claimed to have discovered "the science of mental healing," and she later reflected on how that healing came about:

> I have made what seems to me a discovery. I was fearfully sick. . . . I was thinking about life. . . . Life is simply a form of energy. . . . I told the life in my liver that it was not torpid or inert, but full of vigor and energy. I told the life in my stomach . . . I told the life in my abdomen . . . that it was athrill with the sweet, pure, wholesome energy of God. . . . I went to all the life centers in my body and spoke words of Truth to them.

Such methods are probably neutral in and of themselves. But like so much of the *how-to-listen* instructions, there is no precedent in Scripture. Various forms of meditation or contemplation may be helpful for an individual in the rat race of our hectic lives, but we should not imagine that such rituals offer an individual a more clear understanding of God than an understanding derived from the Bible itself.

Evangelicals would be quick to dismiss Myrtle Fillmore or other New Age gurus, but they have their own steps and principles promoting the art of listening and speaking to God. In *How to Listen to God,* Charles Stanley, television preacher and one-time president of the Southern Baptist Convention, "helps readers rediscover how to distinguish God's voice from all other voices around them." He also instructs readers on "how God gets our attention . . . and how to listen to God." From the story of Adam and Eve, Stanley derives eight principles of what happens when we fail to listen to God:

- We listen to the wrong voices.
- We are easily deceived.
- We express pride and independence of God.
- We make decisions that appeal to the flesh.
- We make excuses for our wrongs.
- We will suffer the consequences.
- Others around us are hurt.
- We miss his very best.

All eight are introduced with "when we fail to listen to God," but they could just as appropriately be introduced with "when we sin." God has already spoken on sin in the Bible, and it complicates matters if people imagine that they must *learn how to listen* to the voice of God for individualized instructions not to sin. God spoke to Adam and Eve, according to the Genesis story, with an audible voice giving very specific and personal instructions. We should not expect such a voice warning us of the consequences of sin.

In *Is that Really You, God?* Loren Cunningham offers "three simple steps that will help you hear God's voice": submit to his lordship, resist the enemy, expect an answer. In addition, he offers several "key points," such as "Allow God to speak to you in the way He chooses," "Confess any unforgiven sin," and "Practice hearing God's voice and it becomes easier." ("It's like picking up the phone and recognizing the voice of your best friend.") He supports his steps and key points with Scripture references, but none of the verses come from a context of how to hear the voice of God. Indeed, those in the Bible who actually *heard* the voice of God needed no instructions, and if it were a prerequisite to have one's sins forgiven before hearing God's voice, Adam and Eve, and Saul on the road to Damascus, among others, would have never received a message. Moreover, it seems presumptuous that we finite beings are in a position to *allow* God to do anything—say nothing of letting him speak "in the way He chooses."

ACCESSING THE MIND OF GOD

Many of the books and articles that offer advice for listening to God appear superficial. Some of those making the most confident claims seem to be the least likely to transmit wisdom to others. In *Hearing God*, Peter Lord says:

> Our God is vitally concerned with reconciliation. . . . As God speaks to you about a brother or sister, you can know his voice by the fact that he will give you thoughts that will work to bring you together. . . . From your heavenly Father, you can expect to hear:
>
> Reasons why you need to get together
> Ways in which you can build bridges to others
> Ways in which you can worship with them
> The worth of our brothers and sisters to him and to us.

Such advice might be helpful, but why is it necessary to introduce it into the discussion of God's speaking apart from Scripture? The Bible itself has much to say on the matter of reconciliation. There are many ways of building bridges in reconciliation. Are we to assume that the specific ones that come to mind are uniquely from God? Such an assumption is presumptuous.

Peter Lord's advice on healing relationships is offered as only one aspect of listening to God in a more general framework. But some individuals whose focus is listening to God specialize in counseling and therapy and emotional *healing* ministries of all kinds. For example, Dave and Linda Olsen, who founded Listening Prayer Ministries in 1992, encourage Christians "to come into dialogue with Jesus for personal intimacy with Him and to teach the church how to let Him be Counselor-Healer of our emotional and spiritual wounds through prayer and healing." Those who practice "listening prayer," according to Dan Schlesinger, enjoy benefits not available to others. "In fact, those who apply listening prayer have an *added advantage* because they simply have immediate access to the mind of God on the matter. In essence, the counselor hears God's words for the counselees."

Leanne Payne counsels people with "repressed memories," identity crises and sexual identity problems through listening prayer. Such counseling suggests that the counsel is not learned from textbooks or based on the ability to recognize emotional distress, but rather is given directly by God. In *The Broken Image,* she acknowledges Agnes Sanford as the "trail-blazer in the art of healing prayer" and describes Sanford's method of "psychological healing" as one that invokes "the Presence of the Lord, asking for his power and love to come in and enable us to discern, and then to break, the oppressing bondages." Such procedures sound profoundly spiritual and thus good in the minds of many people, but claiming one's counsel comes directly from God is potentially dangerous for the counselee.

"Listening to God is the most effective tool we have in our 'healing kit,' " writes Payne, "for by it we know how to collaborate with His Spirit." To illustrate this, she tells a story:

> Agnes Sanford once heard the Spirit tell her not to board a certain plane. She did not and the plane crashed. Later, when she told this story to a group, one woman rather angrily asked her why God would speak to her and not to others. Agnes immediately replied, "Oh, I think He was speaking to all of us. . . . But so few listen."

That God singled out Sanford to escape a plane crash because she was listening and punished others with death because they were not is an arrogant claim. There is only one way, it seems to me, to respond to such circumstances. Rather than claiming that God saved *me* while letting all the others perish, I should humbly thank God for the gift of life and rededicate myself to God in service of others.

There is a downside to the creeping subjectivism that is so prevalent in contemporary Christianity, whether it emerges in sets of rules and steps and principles or through sample case studies. It's all too easy to make presumptuous claims of having a special message from God—especially if a voice is brought forth through the right techniques and methods. Does God speak only at our beck and call? Does God speak only when we appropriate a novel system or twelve-step program? I'm reminded of the lines by Alfred Lord Tennyson:

> Our little systems have their day;
> They have their day and cease to be;
> They are but broken lights of thee,
> And Thou, Oh Lord, art more than they.

MYSTICAL SILENCE

Do we then conclude that it is impossible to hear the voice of God? We should not dismiss the concept of listening altogether, but we need a humility in our claims of hearing God's voice. Frederick Buechner counsels his readers that the time may come when we need "to stop speaking and thinking and reading" and "start watching and listening"—which he confesses is difficult for him because he is an "addicted speaker, thinker, reader." His concept of prayer is primarily that of listening to God: "prayer not as speaking to God, which in a scattered way I do many times a day because I cannot help doing it, but prayer as being deeply silent, as watching and listening for God to speak." He goes on to describe God speaking "through the fathomless quiet of the holy place in the White Tower within us all"—a "quiet holy place in us" that "marks us as God's." As mystical and abstract as this place may be, Buechner does not testify to detailed and personalized messages that God has given him, nor does he counsel other people in their problems with words from God. Rather, he is reflecting on the silent voice of God, and he offers practical advice for spiritual growth:

> What deadens us most to God's presence within us, I think, is the inner dialogue that we are continuously engaged in with ourselves, the endless chatter of human thought. I suspect that there is nothing more crucial to true spiritual *comfort* . . . than being able from time to time to stop that chatter including the chatter of spoken prayer. If we choose to seek the silence of the holy place, or to open ourselves to its seeking, I think there is no surer way than by keeping silent.
>
> God knows I am no good at it, but I keep trying, and once or twice I have been lucky, graced. . . . It is the experience that I think the author of the 131st Psalm is trying to describe.
>
> But I have calmed and quieted my soul,
> like a child quieted at its mother's breast,
> like a child that is quieted is my soul.

Despite all the books and articles and retreats devoted to listening to God or how to hear the voice of God, we ought to be dubious about claims that this is an exercise or skill that can be *learned*. Yet Jesus commands us, "If any man has ears to hear, let him hear" (Mark 4:23). We all must listen and hear, and some people hear differently than others. We should not discredit those for whom *hearing* is a mysterious gift—a gift of listening to silence that some people have and others do not.

In the bestselling novel *The Secret Life of Bees,* August, a beekeeping black woman tries to explain this gift of hearing to Lily, a teenage runaway white girl who is living with her. Speaking of her grandmother, August says, "Well, one time Big Mama told me she went out to the hives on Christmas Eve and heard the bees singing the words of the Christmas story right out of the gospel of Luke." When Lily asks if she really believed it happened, August responds: "Well, yes and no. Some things happen in a literal way, Lily. And then other things, like this one, happen in a not-literal way, but they still happen. Do you know what I mean?" Lily doesn't have a clue. "What I mean is that the bees weren't *really* singing the words from Luke," August continues, "but still, if you have the right kind of ears, you can listen to a hive and hear the Christmas story somewhere inside yourself. You can hear silent things on the other side of the everyday world that nobody else can. Big Mama had those kind of ears. Now, my mother, she didn't really have that gift. I think it skipped a generation."

Hearing God's voice through a White Tower or a bee hive is very different than learning twelve steps for listening. And the voice that is heard may truly be the silent voice of God—not one that easily lends itself to a specific counseling situation, whether our own or someone else's.

7

THE PRAYER CLOSET

God in Silent Conversation

The same evangelical tradition that spurs us on to greater intimacy also invites abuse. "I asked the Lord what to speak on and he said, Don't speak on pride, speak on stewardship." "The Lord told me he wanted a new medical center in this city.". . . The wording implies a kind of voice-to-voice conversation that did not take place, and the fudged report has the effect of creating a spiritual caste that downgrades others' experiences.

PHILIP YANCEY, *REACHING FOR THE INVISIBLE GOD*

As a church historian I often reflect back over the centuries of our Christian heritage and contemplate how the faith has changed over two millennia. A fascinating area of change relates to spirituality and spiritual formation. New Testament spirituality was above all else *active* spirituality. Jesus modeled and preached the active life, as did Paul. That pattern continued on through the early church. In medieval times, as the church became increasingly worldly, spirituality became a vocation that demanded long hours of prayer and contemplation and separation from the world. Spiritual expectations for laypeople and clerics within the church hierarchy were low.

With the Reformation and the emphasis on the priesthood of the believer, however, spiritual formation for the laity was emphasized, particularly in learning the catechism and studying Scripture. During the evangelical revivals of succeeding centuries, the separation between clergy and laity narrowed as experiential religious fervor became a sign of spirituality—one that separated the saved from the lost. This evangelical spirit came to full flowering in the twentieth century with the worldwide spread of Pentecostalism and the charismatic movement.

The further we have moved from the New Testament era the more subjective the faith has become for both Catholics and Protestants. It is not uncommon for the media to report how a pious Catholic saw the figure of the Virgin Mary as the paint dried on the garage, and thousands flock to venerate the image. For Protestants the messages are often verbal, coming in infinite varieties of "two-way" prayer. In these conversations God rarely condemns sin or offers dire warnings of events to come. Far more frequent are the warm messages that focus on specific needs. Those who do not testify to such experiences are easily deemed less spiritual.

GUIDEPOSTS GUIDANCE

There are, of course, cynics. In an article titled "Carrying the Burden of God's Silence," Suzanne Britt writes a parody of this phenomenon. She tells of receiving from a friend a subscription to *Guideposts*—a daily devotional magazine that features what might be termed everyday miracles. "The God of *Guideposts,*" writes Britt, "speaks in complete sentences, telling this golfer to chip rather than putt, suggesting that this housewife bottle her barbeque sauce for the masses and make a million dollars, commanding this entertainer to switch from radio to television." But is this the whole truth, she wonders. What of the times "when God is silent"? Why doesn't *Guideposts* feature stories when there is no "happy ending"—a "story in which God does not make a timely and loquacious appearance at the exact and miraculous moment"? She answers that question with another question: "How many nightclubs would hire a magician whose rabbit never came out of the hat?"

Britt is thought-provoking. If we are presenting God as a magician who pulls what we ask for out of a hat, shouldn't there be consistency? What are we to make of this God who tells a woman to bottle her barbeque sauce, while at the same time allows another woman's bookstore across town to be swept away in a flood?

I recently read a *Guideposts* miracle-prayer story myself. An older missionary couple in Africa tell of being transferred from one mission post to another. Their biggest obstacle was taking their upright piano with them. When they came to a river crossing, the ferry boat driver told them he could not take the piano across. It was the dry season, and the river was too low. They prayed for God's intervention, and not surprisingly the result was rain. The river rose, and the piano was transported safely to the other side.

For some people such stories confirm their faith. But by the same token, when there is no miracle, faith can falter. Not all stories about Africa and rain have a happy ending, and in many cases the stakes are much higher than transporting a piano. This was true for Charles Templeton, an evangelist who worked with Billy Graham in Youth for Christ and then conducted his own evangelistic youth campaigns. After nineteen years he walked away from ministry and the faith. The incident that most separated his belief from his unbelief was seeing a photo in *Life* magazine of an African woman with a dead baby in her arms, "looking up to heaven with the most forlorn expression." Seeing her desperation, he asked himself: "Is it possible to believe that there is a loving or caring Creator when all this woman needed was *rain?*"

For the missionary couple, God sent rain, and the piano proceeded en route. For the mother and a dying baby, there was no rain, and an evangelist lost his faith. The piano stories, however, are the ones we most often feature in Christian literature.

Last year I spoke at a women's conference in Los Angeles. One of my topics was on the silence of God. By coincidence—or providence—one of the other speakers, Marilyn, a pastor's wife, gave a message on conversing with God in prayer. This was not planned. Hers was not a response paper to my session. But the two sessions certainly illustrated the very opposite sides of the issue.

She told a series of stories of how God directly communicates with her on a daily basis from major matters in life to relatively insignificant things. One of her stories, as I recall, related to a little girl she had seen on the school playground who did not have a winter coat. Later that day, Marilyn decided to go to Sears and buy a coat for the girl, but on her way out of the house, God said to her, "Go back to your prayer closet." There, God told her not to go to Sears but to a high-end specialty shop. She questioned God—thinking she could not afford the price. But God again named the shop and told her to go. She went, but to her chagrin the shop was out of girls' coats in that size. She was on her way out of the store, but then turned back and told the clerk of her mission. The clerk informed her that a coat in the size she needed had been selected by a local charity and set aside in the back room for that very purpose. Marilyn graciously accepted the coat and brought it to the little girl.

What's going on here? Marilyn insisted that the voice of God was very clear, perhaps not in audible sounds but nevertheless very clear words coming from the sovereign God of the universe. This woman does not represent some extreme charismatic wing of the church, and she came across as sounding very sincere and credible. Yet I was uncomfortable with her stories, one after another, of how God told her to do this and not do that. I was uncomfortable, and I'm not sure why. Was she just making these stories up? I would not make such an accusation, though I am reminded of an observation C. S. Lewis made about his own spiritual shortcomings: "Those like myself whose imagination far exceeds their obedience . . . easily imagine conditions far higher than we have really reached. If we describe what we have imagined we may make others, and make ourselves, believe that we have really been there—and so deceive both them and ourselves."

As I reflect back and analyze that conference session, it was apparent that the story was not about the little girl. She remained nameless—a poor little girl without a coat. She would have gotten a coat apart from any direct intervention and communication from God—albeit one from Sears. No, this story was about a woman and her prayer closet, and that theme was central to all the stories she told during her hour-long session.

There are two ways to listen to such stories. We can listen and analyze, or we can listen and accept. For those in the latter category, there was only one proposition set forth: direct conversation and communication from God is natural and normal for the Christian life. Indeed, Marilyn told her stories as illustrations of what should be commonplace in the lives of the women who were at that conference. She was not trying to make herself an exception to the rule. If these women—myself included—truly sought God and were open to his voice, we would be able to testify to the same experiences. Our only hindrance was ourselves. God was eager to speak with anyone who would listen.

In fact, Marilyn introduced her prayer partner and told of their similar experiences and how they often shared their stories over the phone. It almost made me wonder if these two women were trying to outdo each other in their stories—a spiritual one-upmanship, so to speak.

Marilyn's story, apart from making other women feel guilty about their lack of spiritual depth, was essentially harmless. Indeed, it was very heartwarming. A little girl without a coat got a coat. Who can fault that? And most people would not find fault. Who would dare challenge a woman who reaches out in love to a stranger, a needy child?

But is it possible that stories like Marilyn's do not serve the cause of Christ? If we think that giving coats to poor children involves supernatural intervention from God, are we less likely to respond to the root causes of such social issues? The underlying problem was not the lack of a coat. There were surely other issues involved, whether parental neglect or alcoholism or racism or unemployment or just plain poverty. As Christians we must be concerned with these systemic problems because Jesus, God incarnate, was concerned. Moreover, even if the root problem were lack of a coat, are we less likely to dig into our own pockets if we are waiting to hear the voice of God on the matter?

I do not know how to explain Marilyn's extraordinary claim to routinely hearing God's voice. I find no comparable instances of God carrying on daily conversations with ordinary individuals in Scripture. In Acts 9 we read of Dorcas who gave clothing to the needy, but there is no mention that such good works were prompted by a voice from God or that the clothing was supplied miraculously. Rather, Dorcas was remembered in life and in death for her charitable deeds. The miracle associated with Dorcas was the astounding account of the apostle Peter's raising her from the dead.

JUST ENOUGH MIRACLE

The greatest miracle in any of our lives would be the evidence that we are truly pious women and men, and a critical part of that piety is serving others by making clothing. The great missionary statesman, E. Stanley Jones has left behind profound wisdom on this matter.

> I believe in miracle, but not too much miracle, for too much miracle would weaken us, make us dependent on miracle instead of our obedience to natural law. Just enough miracle to let us know He is there, but not too much, lest we depend on it when we should depend on our own initiative and on His orderly processes for our development.

How one defines "just enough miracle" is probably a personal matter. What I once thought were *miracles* in my own life, I am no longer certain I could so describe. Indeed, we sometimes use that term too casually. That my granddaughter Kayla has thrived physically and mentally since her birth two-and-a-half months early, following an auto accident, is a wonder of modern medicine. It is true there were praying grandmothers and parents and aunts and uncles and preachers and many more. But the same is true when a pregnant mother was injured generations ago by spooked horses on a wagon train going West, and she lost her baby. The difference, I believe, is not because God responded to what may have been more prayers that were raised for Kayla than the unnamed "preemie" on the frontier, but that Kayla had the advantage of being born in a state-of-the-art neonatal center where medical personnel seemed rather nonchalant about a little one whose birth weight was barely three pounds. Of course we pray for God to guide the hands of the surgeons and the obstetricians, but they often perform "miracles" when no one is praying. Was Kayla's live birth and good development a *miracle* or was it, in the words of Jones, "our own initiative and His orderly processes for our development"?

Marilyn's story of receiving instruction to go to a store where she would receive a coat at no cost is reminiscent of many of the stories of the nineteenth-century *faith* missionaries—perhaps most notably George Müller and Hudson Taylor—as great people of faith who depended on God through prayer alone. God most frequently spoke in terms of money or material goods, providing what was necessary, often at the very last moment. The impression given to outsiders was that the China Inland Mission (CIM, founded by Taylor) had no money worries because it was depending on God by prayer alone. In actuality, however, the leaders of the mission were obsessed with money. In fact, four of the five "principles" of the CIM (requiring no debt, no guaranteed income, dependence on God alone and no solicitation) related to money matters. "The old CIM was surrounded by an aura of secrecy," writes Alvyn Austin. "The biggest secret was money." The records have since shown that while the impression was often given that the CIM was in dire straits financially, in actuality, money was flooding in and the coffers were full.

Neither Taylor nor Müller made their needs known publicly, in order to maintain their vow to live by faith alone. Taylor's creed was unswerving: "When I get out to China, I shall have no claim on anyone for anything; my only claim will be on God. How important, therefore, to learn before leaving England to move man, through God, by prayer alone." But both he and Müller publicized miraculous answers to their prayers, gripping tales of when family and guests (or in Müller's case, orphans) "sat down to the table without a scrap of food in the house; always, providentially, someone would appear at the door with a brace of partridges, a hamper of groceries, or a ton of coal, whatever was needed to survive the next day or week." These were amazing accounts of God's intervention that tugged at the heartstrings of supporters. "These stories, repeated endlessly when the CIM became rich," writes Austin, "reinforced the notion that it was always a poor faith organization."

Truth-telling is a standard that must be the highest priority for all Christians, including those who would profess intimate familiarity with God. Manipulation of the truth is often a thorny temptation for those who would claim God's unique and personal manifestations of blessings. This God who shows special favor cannot be revealed as impotent or weak. What about when the rabbit does not come out of the hat? asks Susanne Britt. We rarely read of stories of orphans starving amidst the miracle stories. Yet it was the photo of a mother and her dead baby in the foreground of sun-scorched land that served as the catalyst for Charles Templeton to walk away from faith. Those who profess to depend on *prayer alone* carry a particular responsibility to eradicate any air of arrogance relating to their intimacy with God—that God uniquely answers their prayers while bypassing the mother with the dead baby in her arms. They must be brutally honest, not only about their own *unanswered* prayers but also about the colossal collective unanswered prayers that only seem to mock the untold numbers of suffering people around the world.

There is great danger in presenting one's spirituality in the light of God's special blessing, a danger of making God in our own image. God becomes the beneficent landlord or banker or Santa Claus. The blessing stories have been at the core of popular missionary biographies of past generations and continue to be the feature of spiritual literature today, especially among charismatics and evangelicals. The massive faith-missions movement spurred by Hudson Taylor and the China Inland Mission opened the floodgates to a miracle-story mentality. In many cases difficult times were reported, but in the end God's *promises* prevailed. This is seen in the mission work of Lettie Cowman and her husband Charles. Like Hudson Taylor, they were also founders of a faith mission, the Oriental Mission Society. Lettie's biographer writes on page after page about money matters: "The days and nights are given to prayer for funds. . . . Funds begin to flow more freely. . . . Soon the funds are gone once more. . . . Things look dark. Funds are falling off at a fearful rate. She goes at once to the bankbook of heaven. . . . Millions of dollars will be needed, but millions of dollars are nothing to God."

Too often we treat God as the "bankbook of heaven." Donald McCullough writes of our vulnerability and temptation to "forsake God for other gods," and this surely includes the god of money. "We will be tempted," he warns, "to create for ourselves gods who will not threaten us with transcendence, gods who will be manifestly useful in a world of confusing voices, and gods who will conform to the contours of our individualistic desires." The God of Scripture "is holy: that is, wholly other than us. . . . A God such as this will never be manageable."

COMPARTMENTALIZED LIVING

If God is not our "bankbook of heaven," then what is the rationale for prayer? I was recently challenged on that subject as a friend questioned me about *what* I prayed for. If I don't pray for sunshine on the day I'm planning to go to the beach, then what *do* I pray for? Much of my praying could be summed up in the opening and closing lines of one of my favorite poems of Emily Dickinson: "My period had come for prayer. . . . I worshipped, did not pray."

I often pray as I walk in my neighborhood—bringing my neighbors names before God and identifying special needs as they come to mind—though surely not as though God doesn't know these needs already. I pray the Lord's prayer, and I pray the words of an old hymn, "Pass me not O gentle Savior, / Hear my humble cry." I pray prayers of thanksgiving dozens of times a day, sometimes almost unconsciously. But I also pray prayers of thanksgiving very consciously, especially after I was challenged by Ruth Graham. She endured heartbreaking trials as a mother, and many times she offered pleading prayers of anguish, particularly regarding her sons. One night she was lying awake worried about Ned. She turned on the light and opened her Bible to Philippians 4: "Be careful for nothing, but in every thing by prayer and supplication with thanksgiving let your requests be made known unto God" (v. 6 KJV). In that moment her prayer life was transformed: "Suddenly I realized the missing ingredient to my prayers had been thanksgiving. So I sat there and thanked God for all that Ned was and all he meant to me through the years." Such prayers of thanksgiving changed Ruth Graham—and have changed me—perhaps far more than they have necessarily changed the circumstances. And that, after all, is a key to prayer. The words on the plaque say "Prayer Changes Things," but a more fitting inscription might be "Prayer Changes Me," most specifically in my relationship with God. Prayer is spiritual formation, communion with and dependence on God.

My prayers today are far less regimented than they were in the past. I used to pray through lists during a specified time that I set aside—though sometimes feeling like a lesser Christian because my *devotions* were not slotted in first thing in the morning. I can still hear the indictment of Bill, a faithful stalwart at Whitneyville Bible Church: "If you can't find time for God before breakfast, you shouldn't eat breakfast or any meal until you find the time." But I was not a morning person. I was in the habit of giving God devotional time before going to bed.

In *Seeing God in the Ordinary,* Michael Frost challenges Christians not to compartmentalize their lives, with the sacred in one area and the secular or *profane* in another. "This version of Christianity," he writes, taking a cue from H. Richard Niebuhr, "maintains the distinction by placing one *over and above* the other." Attending a religious meeting or spending time in private prayer is perceived as *over and above* walking your child to school.

> Our spiritual life (which we speak of as a component of our experience distinct from everything else) involves us in a quest to be ever calling the sacred down into the ordinariness of this world. We pray for God to be with us in our job interview as if God wouldn't otherwise show up. We invite God into our church meeting as we would an honored guest arriving fashionably late. . . . Such a view flattens the power of the gospel message. It becomes a grid for determining where and when God is at work in our world.

What then is prayer? Is it just a little routine we repeat like a mantra? Is it a ceremonial procedure that gets the ball rolling before we get down to the real business at hand? I'm sometimes amused and perplexed by how rigid we are in our prayer habits—especially in Christian organizations. I've been in some settings where failure to say a prayer before a committee meeting would be perceived as ill-mannered as failing to curtsey before the queen. And saying grace before a meal is an obligatory ritual in some circles. I am sometimes in the company of people who come into a lunch room where they individually and silently bow their heads in prayer over their lunch bag. That's OK. But when I think of saying grace, I think of a communal affair, of holding hands, and perhaps saying it after the meal is over. Or maybe saying grace means not saying an *official* prayer at all. There is much to be said for G. K. Chesterton's practice of prayer, or grace:

> You say grace before meals. All right, but I say grace before the concert and the opera, and grace before the play and the pantomime, and grace before I open a book, and grace before sketching, painting, swimming, fencing, boxing, walking, playing, dancing and grace before I dip the pen in ink.

If Chesterton said grace before a concert, I would imagine he applauded at the end of the concert—a gesture that might appropriately apply at the end of an interminably long prayer. Elie Wiesel tells how Toscanini, the famous conductor, visited the Grand Canyon while on tour in America. As he gazed in awe at the beauty of God's creation, he first paused in silence and then burst out in applause. O that our prayers might be such—spontaneous appreciation for the splendor and for the simple things in life.

Prayer, it seems, has become a topic—like spiritual formation in general—that is deemed so sacred it cannot be touched. It is in a realm that is beyond everyday life. But prayer is prayer. It is our way of talking with God, and in and of itself it possesses no uniquely sanctified quality. I am reminded of a story about the outspoken nineteenth-century evangelist D. L. Moody. He was presiding over an evangelistic campaign in England during which time an invited guest was offering a seemingly unending prayer. Moody finally interrupted and said to the large gathering, "Let us all join in singing a chorus while our brother finishes his prayer."

When prayer becomes too sacred it loses its savor. And not only does prayer become too sacred, but it is often turned into a complicated procedure—something that we *learn* to do or something that becomes more effective as we develop and perfect our skills. I have often heard the phrase, "She's a real prayer warrior." Well, perhaps. But should prayer even be perceived in such terms, as in storming heaven. Yet that very phraseology is sometimes employed in especially difficult circumstances, as in when a friend has been critically injured in an auto accident. Does God more likely respond favorably when we storm heaven, or when someone who has expertise in praying comes in on the case?

In recent years there have been many regional "concerts of prayer," especially for missions. These gatherings often feature special speakers and PowerPoint presentations and statistical analyses of unreached people around the world. They are presumed to be more effective in swaying God than were the old-fashioned Wednesday night church prayer meetings. In my youth and young adult years, prayer wasn't fashionable. Today, prayer has almost taken a glitzy turn. Books and websites abound. Intercessory prayer is the brand that sells. Intercessory prayer is not to be confused with your ordinary garden-variety prayer. It stands out for its sense of power and urgency, and is promoted for its high rate of effectiveness. In fact, Google offers more than 100,000 sites on intercessory prayer alone, with prayer webrings and prayer networks and prayer-warrior directories—and even a Prayer Bear ministry.

Prayer, in much of the contemporary literature, is viewed as something to be learned—something at which one becomes proficient. In *Celebration of Discipline,* Richard Foster writes that "Real prayer is something we learn." His point seems to be that the main reason our prayers are not answered in the affirmative is because we have not properly learned how to pray. "One of the most critical aspects in learning to pray for others is to get in contact with God so that his life and power can flow through us into others," he writes. "Often people pray and pray with all the faith in the world, but nothing happens. Naturally, they were not tuned in to God." Like many other writers on prayer, Foster emphasizes the necessity of *listening.* "Listening to the Lord is the first thing, the second thing, and the third thing necessary for successful intercession." Such advice is not an obvious conclusion one could draw from Scripture, nor is Foster's counsel that prayer for major concerns demand more proficiency than prayer for little things. "In physical matters," he writes, "we always tend to pray for the most difficult situations first: terminal cancer or multiple sclerosis. But when we listen [to God], we will learn the importance of beginning with smaller things like colds or earaches. Success in small corners of life gives us authority in the larger matters. If we are still, we will learn not only who God is, but how his power operates."

That a beginner in prayer should start with colds and work up to cancer is simply not a biblical concept.

JABEZ OR JESUS?

The most recent bestselling treatise on prayer is *The Prayer of Jabez* by Bruce Wilkinson. Its popularity was based in part on our near universal tendency toward self-absorption. And this tendency is a common element in prayer: what Bill Hybels refers to as "the 'Please God' syndrome. 'Please God, give me . . . help me . . . comfort me . . . strengthen me. . . .'" This "Please God" syndrome, of course, is not blatantly selfish. Indeed, it is marked by a concern for others: "Please God, bless me so that I can bless others." In *The Prayer of Jabez,* based on one verse in the Old Testament (1 Chronicles 4:10), Wilkinson develops a philosophy of prayer:

> If Jabez had worked on Wall Street, he might have prayed, "Lord, increase the value of my investment portfolios." When I talk to presidents of companies, I often talk to them about this particular mind-set. When Christian executives ask me, "Is it right for me to ask God for more business?" my response is, "Absolutely!" If you're doing your business God's way, it's not only right to ask for more, but He is waiting for you to ask. Your business is the territory God has entrusted to you.

Wilkinson states the purpose of the book in the preface: "I want to teach you how to pray a daring prayer that God always answers. It is brief—only one sentence with four parts—and tucked away in the Bible, but I believe it contains the key to a life of extraordinary favor with God." Is this single verse an illumination on communication with God? Does it provide the key to unlocking the secret of prayer?

It is difficult to make airtight generalizations about prayer in the Bible. Yet many people are tempted to take one story or one verse and turn it into a particular philosophy of prayer. But prayer is a subject that is filled with as many apparent contradictions as is any topic in the Bible. It is, however, safe to say that prayer as a *learned* discipline for the Christian is rooted in the Lord's Prayer, not the prayer of Jabez. Jesus offered that prayer in response to his disciples' request, "Lord, teach us to pray." Even the most cursory reflection on that prayer reminds us that God is the focus: "Hallowed be *Thy* name. *Thy* kingdom come. *Thy* will be done." There is, of course, a request for daily bread and an acknowledgment of sin and temptation. But the end of that short prayer, which can be repeated in twenty seconds, returns to the focus on God: "*Thine* is the kingdom, and the power, and the glory for ever. Amen."

Those who emphasize *power* in prayer are often making reference to the power that human beings can wield through prayer. But the power spoken of in the Lord's Prayer belongs to God alone, and there is no indication of human power through prayer, unless the humble request for daily bread is misinterpreted as power. What then do we do with such offers from Jesus as, "Ask and it will be given to you" (Matthew 7:7)? The varied interpretations of those words are far too numerous to recount in this volume, but we should not assume that they are to be taken at face value. Jesus often spoke in hyperbole—as in, *if your eye offends you, pluck it out*—and this offer to give all that we ask should be interpreted in like manner. Indeed, Jesus did not grant all requests in his own earthly ministry.

Prayer, above all else, should be spoken with humility—not with audaciousness or a confidence that we have an ability to pull strings to manipulate the God of the universe. Some of the most powerful prayers in the Bible are those that reflect a deep sense of humility. "God, have mercy on me, a sinner," the publican pleaded, smiting his breast. "Lord, I believe. Help my unbelief," was the self-effacing prayer of a man whose only request was that his daughter be healed. The prayer of Jesus on the cross, "My God, my God, why have you forsaken me?" is often our own humble cry of anguish, and "Father, forgive them" serves as a pattern of humility when we are wronged.

Not only should prayer be offered in an attitude of humility, but it should be something we speak about in an attitude of humility. We easily feel second-rate when we hear the accounts of the prayer giants of past generations or even those today who tell of impressive prayer lives. When we compare ourselves to them, it is tempting to exaggerate our own piety so as not to appear slothful in our spirituality.

ORA ET LABORA

Most of us struggle in the area of prayer, and our pretense often falls far short of reality. And I speak here not just of amateurs in the pews. What about our priests and ministers? Do they win the medals in the Olympic prayer competition events? Bill Hybels, senior pastor of Willow Creek Community Church, certainly did not. He confesses that as a pastor his prayer life had been "amazingly weak" for many years. "It wasn't that I hadn't wanted to pray," he writes. "I always had good intentions. I *tried* to pray. But I would get down on my knees and say, 'Dear God . . .' and in five seconds my mind would be in outer space. I would start thinking of people I hadn't seen in years, making up solutions for problems that didn't exist." The failure was particularly frustrating because in other areas he had a "tremendous ability to concentrate." But not with prayer. "Prayer did me in every time. I would hear people speak of praying for four hours, and I would feel terrible knowing I couldn't pray for four minutes."

A friend's suggestion that he write out his prayers made a difference:

"Though I've been a Christian for years," he testifies, "I never privately worshiped God on a consistent basis—until I started writing out my prayers."

Henri Nouwen's confession is similar to Hybels. We might assume that as a Catholic priest and spiritual writer, he would model an exemplary prayer life. "So what about my life of prayer? Do I like to pray? Do I want to pray? Do I spend time praying?" he asks. "Frankly, the answer is no to all three questions. After sixty-three years of life and thirty-eight years of priesthood, my prayer seems as dead as a rock. . . . The truth is that I do not feel much, if anything, when I pray." But then Nouwen asks a most provocative and penetrating question: "Is the death of my prayer the end of my intimacy with God or the beginning of a new communion, beyond words, emotions, and bodily sensations?"

In God's eyes, the death of Nouwen's prayer life may have been a very old *communion* of which he was not even conscious. The best prayers are ones that are so entwined with action that it's impossible to tell where the *praying* ends and the *doing* begins. Nouwen was a man of action, a man of good deeds, as he sought to meet the needs of the profoundly handicapped at the Daybreak community. The Latin phrase *ora et labora*—pray and work—is associated with the Benedictine rule (and the rule for many monastic communities). We know from the epistle of James that faith without works is dead, but also of prayer. Prayer without works is dead. Indeed the burden of *answered* prayer falls, at least in part, on us.

A powerful example of this in relation to *ora et labora* comes from Hudson Taylor. Although he seemed often obsessed with money in later years, there is a story of answered prayer in his early ministry that bears repeating again and again. "The Prayer of Taylor"—as opposed to *The Prayer of Jabez*—is a model for all Christians. It is an extraordinary illustration of how our prayer life should function, how we truly are "co-laborers with God."

Before he began his mission work in China, Hudson Taylor was an independent lay evangelist among those "in the lowest part of" London. One night as Taylor was preparing to return home, a man accosted him, pleading for a home visit. His wife was very ill and his children were hungry. He had asked a priest to come and pray, but he could not afford the eighteen-pence charge. The man did not even have money to buy bread for the next meal. Taylor followed him to the dilapidated tenement building, up the rickety steps and down the dark hallway to the dimly lit room. It was a wretched sight, seeing the woman lying on rags with a newborn infant at her side and hungry children huddled close by.

Taylor tried to offer some words of encouragement, but all he could think of was the half-crown weighing down his pocket. He had just been paid, and he had to stretch it to subsist for the next month. *If only I had some shillings and pennies,* he thought, *I could give them something for their next meal.* "Something within me cried, 'You hypocrite! Telling these unconverted people about a kind and loving Father in heaven, and not prepared yourself to trust him without half a crown.' "

Anxious to get his visit over with and leave, he knelt to pray. "But no sooner had I opened my lips with, 'Our Father who art in heaven,' than conscience said within, 'Dare you mock God? Dare you kneel down and call him "Father" with that half-crown in your pocket?'" Without finishing his prayer, Taylor got up, so distraught, that the man wondered if something was wrong. He reached into his pocket and handed the man the half-crown, instructing him to buy medication and food. God had answered the prayer before it was finished. And not just for the family, but for Taylor himself: "And how the joy came back in full flood tide to my heart. . . . Not only was the poor woman's life saved, but my life as fully realized had been saved too."

Some years ago when that story was fresh in my mind, friends asked for prayer regarding their finances. The husband had just been laid off, and they were unable to meet the mortgage payment. I prayed, but then stopped mid-sentence. I went to the phone and called, asking how much their monthly payment was, and then made out a check for that amount and stuck it in the mail. I'm convinced that is exactly what Paul means when he says we are "co-laborers with God." How dare I pray to God to meet their financial needs when I have the ability to reach for that half-crown in my pocket even while I am praying for them?

There has been a great emphasis on intercessory prayer in recent years. Prayer is *work*, Henry and Richard Blackaby insist. It is a battle. "The tragedy regarding intercession," they write, "is that God often looks in vain for those willing to enter the deep levels of prayer required in interceding for others. . . . Few are willing to pay the price to intercede at the deepest spiritual levels."

I believe that the price most people are unwilling to pay is not the agonizing and writhing and pleading with God to do something, but rather reaching into their own pocket for the half-crown.

8

GOD IN THE HANDS OF AN ANGRY SINNER

Silence and the Fairness Issue

But whether it is the road to Golgotha on which we walk, or the road to Babylon, or the road to Auschwitz, or the road that leads to our own death, only silence answers our prayer. In that silence, death casts its shadow over more than just our life. It casts its shadow over our faith as well. Where is God while we suffer and die?

G. TOM MILAZZO, *THE PROTEST AND THE SILENCE*

Where Is God While We Suffer and Die? would be an appropriate title for a commentary on the book of Job. This portion of Scripture—all forty-two chapters of Job—speaks more profoundly on the matter of God's silence than does any other book of the Bible. Amidst all his suffering, Job could not even find God. He was distraught. He lamented his futile search:

> But if I go to the east, he is not there;
> If I go to the west, I do not find him
> When he is at work in the north, I do not see him;
> When he turns to the south, I catch no glimpse of him. (Job 23:8-9)

The book of Job is filled with lamentation and anger and venting rage over God's injustice. We find this theme also in many of the psalms, nearly half of which are "lamentations of God's apparent abandonment" and "cries of complaint to a God who seems indifferent to Israel's wretched plight."

Anger and silence often go together. One spouse, out of anger, gives the other the silent treatment, and the other is angry about the silence. God is sometimes accused of giving the *silent treatment,* not being simply oblivious to the needs of humankind or to the needs of a particular individual but rather of purposely turning away in silence.

In *A Grief Observed,* C. S. Lewis confesses the deep sense of abandonment he experienced after the death of his wife. "Meanwhile, where is God?" he angrily inquired. "Go to him when your need is desperate, when all other help is vain, and what do you find? A door slammed in your face, and a sound of bolting and double bolting on the inside. After that, silence. You may as well turn away. The longer you wait, the more emphatic the silence will become." Who is this God of silence? How does one counter such seeming callousness? Lewis, in his grief, had his own way of revenge: "All that stuff about the cosmic sadist was not so much the expression of thought as of hatred. I was getting from it the only pleasure a man in anguish can get: the pleasure of hitting back."

God slams the door and then is silent. Is God a cosmic sadist? Job wonders about that as he bitterly expresses anger concerning the unfairness and the silence of God. The closest expression of Job-like anger that I have encountered in contemporary terminology comes from the pen of Arthur Krystal, in an article in the *American Scholar.* Like Job, he vents his rage at God's injustice.

> This God, the God of the book, . . . is a stunted God, who apparently has nothing better to do than hang around our teeny section of the galaxy and amuse Himself at our expense. . . . You may not be bothered by a hands-on God who lets loose with massacres and disease, but I am. . . . If such a God exists, why would I want to

spend eternity with the likes of Him? And if He exists, I hope I shall have the courage to tell Him off. Just because I may end up acknowledging Him doesn't mean I have to approve of Him. Call this—with apologies to Jonathan Edwards—my "God in the Hands of an Angry Sinner" sermon.

And Job, shocking as it may seem to modern-day evangelicals, does have the courage to "tell God off."

RAGE AGAINST GOD

Job's short bio is summed up in the first three verses of the book:

> In the land of Uz there lived a man whose name was Job. This man was blameless and upright; he feared God and shunned evil. He had seven sons and three daughters, and he owned seven thousand sheep, three thousand camels, five hundred yoke of oxen and five hundred donkeys, and had a large number of servants. He was the greatest man among all the people of the East. (Job 1:1-3)

In verse 9 Satan argues that Job fears God merely because he is blessed with such abundance. So God allows Satan to test Job. All that Job possesses is taken away from him—including his health. He is stricken with painful sores from the soles of his feet to the top of his head, and his wife tells him to curse God and die.

The chapters that follow are conversations between Job and his three friends, who insist that he would not be suffering had he not sinned against God. Job argues with them, and to them he spells out his complaints against God. Then in chapter 10, Job speaks directly to God—telling him off, so to speak.

> I loathe my very life;
> therefore I will give free rein to my complaint
> and speak out in the bitterness of my soul. . . .

Does it please you to oppress me,
  to spurn the work of your hands,
  while you smile on the schemes of the wicked? . . .
Are your days like those of a mortal
  or your years like those of a man,
that you must search out my faults
  and probe my sin—
though you know that I am not guilty
  and that no one can rescue me from your hand?
Your hands shaped me and made me.
  Will you now turn and destroy me?
  Remember that you molded me like clay.
Will you now turn me to dust again? . . .

Why then did you bring me out of the womb?
  I wish I had died before any eye saw me.
If only I had never come into being,
  or had been carried straight from the womb to the grave! . . .
  Turn away from me so I can have a moment's joy
before I go to the place of no return,
  to the land of gloom and deep shadow,
to the land of deepest night,
  of deep shadow and disorder,
  where even the light is like darkness. (Job 10:1-9, 18-22)

Job's friends certainly recognized his anger. In chapter 15, one of his friends is horrified by Job's shocking words: "Why do your eyes flash, / so that you vent your rage against God / and pour out such words from your mouth?" (vv. 12-13). Here we have a picture of God in the hands of an angry sinner.

Job's anger stems from the terrible injustice he is feeling. And despite the metaphors of God's anger as gnashing and burning, God's response is primarily that of silence. It is as though God is ignoring him, simply refusing to listen. Doug Frank writes of this in contemporary terms: "I have a friend who, for many months, has mourned a terrible loss. . . . He has suffered ceaseless waves of grief and rage. . . . He has seen the Nothing. He . . . has flung 'I never knew the man' into the face of a thunderingly silent God. The words of the flesh and blood Jesus, 'My God, why have you forsaken me?', are his words too."

Job, unlike Jesus and others who surrender to the silence of God, is confrontational. Nothing raises the blood pressure more than two sides pitted against each other in a court case, and that is exactly what he is mulling over in his mind. In chapter 9, he wishes God were a man

> that we might confront each other in court.
> If only there were someone to arbitrate between us,
> to lay his hand upon us both,
> someone to remove God's rod from me. (vv. 32-34)

In that way he would force God to listen. He is convinced that any fair person—any honest judge—would take his side. Time and again, Job uses the imagery of a court of law as the only forum upon which to demand justice from God.

In chapter 13, God becomes the judge, as Job laments: "I desire to speak to the Almighty and to argue my case with God." Again in that chapter, he says, "Now that I have prepared my case, I know I will be vindicated" (vv. 3, 16).

Toward the end of the book, after Job's three friends finish speaking, another angry man enters the fray—Elihu. He is not only angry with Job, but he is also angry with the three friends for their inability to refute Job. Some commentators have suggested that this last speaker has little new to offer. I disagree. Elihu speaks more pointedly than do the others to the issue of the silence of God. In chapter 34, he says of God: "But if he remains silent, who can condemn him? If he hides his face, who can see him" (v. 29). In some ways, that says it all. What if God were to give a response to the problem of pain? the problem of evil? Would the answers solve the problem? Wouldn't answers be a setup for condemnation? "But if he remains silent, who can condemn him?"

What Job endures defies human logic. His pain and loss simply make no sense at all. God makes no effort to make sense out of the senseless. And at the end of the book there is silence.

If the book of Job tells us anything, it is that we should not seek to make sense out of the apparent injustices of life. Like God, we should remain silent. Though Job laments the silence of God, he certainly prefers that silence to the flood of words from his friends. Barbara Brown Taylor has aptly characterized these friends: "In their ministerial anxiety, they are like flies buzzing around him on his dung heap. If they would just shut up. . . . They are in his way. They are in God's way. They are trying to insert themselves between the silence of God and the one for whom the silence is intended."

In the end God offers no resolution to the problem of pain. God says nothing about justice and injustice. And Job lived happily ever after—never again, we assume, shaking his fist at a silent God. But the story of God in the hands of an angry sinner has been repeated infinite times in the generations since Job. The book of Job stands as an everlasting monument to God's acceptance of anger—over and above, I would argue, apologetical arguments to explain away the problem of pain. The story of Job is a universal story that serves as a backdrop for our very personal accounts of pain and suffering.

C. S. Lewis offers reflections on the story of Job as it applied to the circumstances of his friend Charles Williams, whose faith was only matched by his pessimism and skepticism. If that side of him, he conjectured "wanted to carry its hot complaints to the very Throne, even that, he felt, would be a permitted absurdity. . . . Job's impatience had been approved. His apparent blasphemies had been accepted." Williams had rightly concluded that God's righteous indignation was aimed at the "comforters," the "sort of people," he scoffed, "who wrote books on the Problem of Pain."

For Christians the book of Job, while viewed with interest, is not seen as foundational to the faith. For Jews, on the other hand, the heated interchange between Job and God pierces to the very core of their faith. Rabbi David Wolpe, tells of participating on a CNN panel with a priest and a Muslim cleric, who both spoke of love as the heart of the faith. Wolpe relates that he spoke of love as well, but that he also spoke of anger. In a meditation on this aspect of faith, he points out that "Yisrael means wrestling with God," and goes on to say, "We are God wrestlers. . . . Don't tell me we should not blame God since . . . God gave us free will and we are culpable. . . . To be angry with God, as Elie Wiesel has taught us, means to be in relationship to God. I feel God in my fury and love God in my bewilderment."

Some of the hottest complaints against God do indeed come from the pen of Jewish writers, particularly Elie Wiesel. In his personal memoir *Night,* he tells of the horrors of being deported to Auschwitz at age fourteen, a boy devoted to his Jewish faith. At one point he was with his father crowded among other prisoners. "Someone began to recite the Kaddish, the prayer for the dead," writes Wiesel. "I do not know if it has ever happened before, in the long history of the Jews, that people have ever recited the prayer for the dead for themselves. . . . 'May His Name be blessed and magnified . . .' whispered my father." It was then that Wiesel, for the first time, experienced anger and revolt against God: "Why should I bless His Name? The Eternal, Lord of the Universe, the All-Powerful and Terrible, was silent. What had I to thank him for?" The nightmare seemed unending as the atrocities filled both his waking hours and his sleep. "Never shall I forget that nocturnal silence which deprived me, for all eternity, of the desire to live. Never shall I forget those moments which murdered my God and my soul and turned my dreams to dust. Never shall I forget these things, even if I am condemned to live as long as God Himself. Never."

The Holocaust was a watershed between belief and unbelief for many Jewish people. For some, however, there seemed to be no choice but to go on believing—as was apparently true of the anonymous individual whose message was scrawled on a wall in a death camp:

I believe in the sun
even when it is not
shining.

I believe in love
even when not
feeling it.

I believe in God
even when He is silent.

Yet there were many whose belief in the sun and love returned, but not their belief in God. In ancient times God's silence did not necessarily negate God's presence. "Even in exile and suffering, confidence in the presence and reality of God endured," writes Tom Milazzo. "Only in our time was this confidence broken. And with its passing, the question of the reality of God became very real for us."

How do we carry on in our faith in times of great sorrow and pain? If we truly believe in a personal God, is there any alternative but indescribable anger—so fierce that it can no longer acknowledge a *personal* God who is supposed to have the power to prevent such searing anguish? Hans Küng, unlike many theologians, makes no effort to explain God in times like this, but he does offer a way for us to continue to recognize God as God: "Yes, to cling to him even in an absolutely desperate situation, simply empty and burnt out, when all prayer dies out and not a word can be spoken: *a fundamental trust of the most radical kind,* which does not externally appease anger and indignation but encompasses and embraces them."

NOT OUR KIND OF FOLKS

Some people insist that there is no place for a Christian to argue with God. In *Hearing God's Voice* the Blackabys pose this question: "Is it OK to wrestle with God's will and to express my anger at God as long as I am being honest about how I feel?" They respond: "The short answer is no! . . . A person who argues with God obviously does not really know God. . . . If you truly know God as he is—holy, almighty, perfect and just—will you be inclined to wrestle with him? Not likely."

John Piper is even more explicit. In response to the question "Is it ever right to be angry with God?" he responds on his website: "It is never, ever, ever, right to be angry with God." He goes on to say that if a person sins by being angry with God, that person should surely confess the sin, but that any anger against God is absolutely wrong. He cites Jonah 4:9 and Job 42:6. God asks Jonah, "Do you have a right to be angry about the vine?" and Jonah responds that he does, that he is "angry enough to die." God then expresses concern for Nineveh, and that is how the narrative ends. God asks, "Should I not be concerned about that great city?" (v. 11).

In the case of Job, it is true that he said to God, "I despise myself and repent in dust and ashes." Such language may indicate that Job regarded his anger with God as sin. But the context of the passage makes it clear that God is not angry with Job. Rather God is angry with Job's three self-righteous friends. In the verse following Job's repentance, God said to Eliphaz: "I am angry with you and your two friends, because you have not spoken of me what is right, as my servant Job has." In neither case does God say that the anger expressed by Jonah or Job is sin. Job had spoken of God's anger much earlier in the narrative. In Job 9:5, for example, he says of God: "He moves mountains without their knowing it /

and overturns them in his anger." But there is no indication that any such display of anger on God's part was prompted by Job's anger.

Anger comes in many forms. In some cases it comes in the fire of indignation, as in shaking one's fist at God. In other cases it comes in the form of the silent treatment or in the form of beaten-down resignation.

"I recently learned that I have terminal cancer." These were the words of the late Claire Hahn, a woman who left the convent and became an English literature professor at Fordham University. "I had encountered such crises as second hand many times in the characters of English literature," she writes, "but now I was . . . face up against my own." How does one relate to God in such circumstances? Can we love God under such conditions? Does God fully identify with our vulnerability and pain?

> In the same hospital room with me was a woman, a black lady who had both legs amputated. When her bandages were changed, the pain was excruciating and she cried out. The nurse said to her, "Put your faith in the Lord." The woman replied, "When you do that, you get hit," and then asked me, "Do you have faith in the Lord?" "Well, yes," I replied. "So do I," she said, "but do you like the Lord?" "No," I confessed, "I do not like the Lord." "I don't either. God's not our kind of folks."

God's not our kind of folks. This was the cry of Job. *If only* God were a man, then he could bring him to court. He could put God on trial. But God is God, and he's not our kind of folks—except the incarnate Christ who suffered every temptation, every indignity, every excruciating pain (and more) than we have.

For some people, God *is* our kind of folks. God is toying with us like a factory foreman with just enough power and sadistic energy to browbeat the underlings fearing for their jobs. Some respond in anger; others are more nonchalant. Tevye, in *Fiddler on the Roof* seems to take the idea of God toying with him in stride—with no visible outpouring of anger:

"Dear God, did you have to make my poor old horse lose his shoe just before the Sabbath? That wasn't nice. It's enough you pick on me. . . . What have you got against my horse? Sometimes I think when things are too quiet up there, You say to Yourself: 'Let's see, what kind of mischief can I play on my friend Tevye?'"

Tevye's lightheartedness aside, there is no satisfactory answer to the anger that individuals often express toward God. God did not answer the problem of pain, nor should we. But it is no small thing that the Christian faith alone allows us to glimpse a suffering God. The refrain of an old hymn says it all in one profound question: "Amazing love! How can it be / that thou, my God, shouldst die for me?" I thought of those words some years ago when I was listening to a young African American man speak before a large audience. He was telling how he had been raised in a poor city neighborhood by his single mother and professed faith in Christ as a young boy in a little Pentecostal storefront church. But as he grew to adulthood, he became more and more conscious of the embedded racism in all the Christian churches in town. They were hypocritical in their professed love for the people of all nations while they ignored the poor and needy in their own city. He walked away—from the cross to the crescent—from Christianity to Islam. The Christians and their God, he fumed, had done nothing for him. The Muslims had given him a faith community that he had never known before. He raged on and on, citing one comparison after another, with one last jab. He was no longer worshiping a God who died on a cross. He was worshiping Allah, and Allah hadn't died.

There lies the difference. Allah did not die on a cross for our sins. Jesus did. Only Jesus could know the suffering this young man had endured as a little boy growing up in poverty without a dad. It is only of Jesus that we can ask, *How can it be that Thou, my God, shouldst die for me?*

John Mark Hicks tells the story of his severely impaired and terminally ill fifteen-year-old son Joshua. He had began objecting to boarding a school bus in the morning, an activity he had previously looked forward to. Then one day, as he was seeing his son off, Hicks heard other children ridiculing him for his having to wear diapers and for his inability to walk straight. He was outraged, wanting "to take some of those older kids aside and heap some abuse of my own on them." He was angry. How could God allow this to happen? There was no answer to his problem of pain, but there was consolation.

> I went to my office and poured my heart before [God]. Why was my son born with this condition? Why are others permitted to inflict pain upon the innocent? Somewhere in the middle of that complaint, in the middle of the lament, I became intensely aware that my complaint had been heard. . . . It was as if God said to me, "I understand . . . they treated my Son that way, too." In that moment God provided a comfort that I cannot yet explain but one that I still experience in my heart.

THE TRIUNE GOD

For Christians, as with Jews and Muslims, there is no answer to the problem of pain. But Christians, unlike all others, find their identity in Christ who in the midst of suffering and death, cried out, "My God, my God, why have you forsaken me?" It is the only response to the silence of God, and if it sounds too much like a cry of anger, so be it. God's condemnation is reserved for those who would stand in to offer answers.

Venting one's anger at God, as Job demonstrated, is surely no sign of unbelief. The most obvious indicator of unbelief is indifference, and indifference is the most common response to God's silence. We are schooled to believe, as the Blackabys and John Piper admonish us, that anger directed at God is sin. So when God is silent in the face of our Job-like misfortunes, we too easily walk away in apathy, reasoning that a silent God is no better than no God at all. But a silent God is not a statue.

A silent God is not an unmoved mover. A silent God is no mere ground of being. A silent God is the only deity we have—our triune God: *Father,* who has spoken in times past, through the prophets; *Son,* who walked among us, leaving behind a sermon, a prayer and many parables; and *Holy Spirit,* whose groanings are more comprehensible than our own words in the language of heaven.

God—this God we worship, this God in whom we live and move and have our being—is a silent God. But surely no less real. Our response may at times be one of anger, a response God not merely tolerates but accepts as a sign of engagement. This response shows far more humility than when we mere mortals presume to defend (or speak for) God. But anger should not be our natural response to God's silence. The natural response is acceptance and a feeling of security that an infant senses—snuggled close to the mother's breast, the only sound is that of her breathing.

9

"SILENT NIGHT, HOLY NIGHT"

The Incarnation and the Silence of God

Silent night, holy night, . . .
Sleep in heavenly peace.

JOSEF MOHR, "SILENT NIGHT"

How silently, how silently,
The wondrous gift is given.

PHILLIPS BROOKS, "O LITTLE TOWN OF BETHLEHEM"

Giving birth is not a silent enterprise. I know. I was there at the births of my son and my granddaughter. And all the stories I've been told about childbirth confirm that *silence* simply does not describe the scene. The mother's moaning, the clipped phrases of those assisting, the baby's cry and the joyous exclamations (if all goes well) are all part of the experience. So too that first Christmas. With all that we do not know about specific circumstances in the stable or cave, we surely must assume that it wasn't silent. There were noises—all kinds of noises—that night. For an aspiring Austrian poet-priest, however, "Noisy night, holy night" simply would not have worked.

But in many ways that incredibly eventful night was a silent night. God incarnate came silently to this earth. Though heralded by angels, the birth was hardly newsworthy. It occurred under the cover of night in a shed in a nondescript village among poor folks—*our kind of folks.* And they weren't even locals, whose baby would be listed among the births in the Bethlehem *Weekly Gazette.* God the Son had come a long way, further than Nazareth, to be born, and no one seemed to notice.

THE HIDDENNESS OF GOD

Jesus grew up incognito and remained so most of his life. Where was Jesus for eighteen years, between the time he discussed theology with priests and elders in the temple and when he began his public ministry? Some New Age writers claim he was traveling through Persia and on to India, where he studied with Hindu gurus and came back to Galilee with his new beliefs in karma and reincarnation. The only problem with that theory is that Jesus never taught Hindu concepts. But the theory fills in the gap of those eighteen *silent* years. Well-meaning Christians through the centuries have likewise sought to fill up Jesus' early years with activity, miracles and legends of all sorts. Yet Scripture tells us that when Jesus did begin his public ministry, people were surprised because they knew him simply as the carpenter's son—and only that. God was silent, even when taking on the human form.

The promised return, the second coming of Jesus, will be in power and great glory, but no such power and glory defined the first coming. In fact, in many respects the incarnation of the Son of God is not slam-dunk apologetical proof for the presence of God. God's silence is woven tightly into the very fabric of the incarnation. Except for some impressive public miracles, the presence of God on this planet was not evident to the naked eye, and it was missed by the vast majority of the population of the first-century world. It would be easy to argue that the work of Satan was more apparent during that short span of years than the work of Jesus. "The Gospels assert that Jesus . . . was none other than God's own Son, dispatched from heaven to lead the fight against evil," writes Philip Yancey. "With that mission in view . . . why not tackle a few macro-problems like earthquakes and hurricanes, or perhaps the whole sinister swarm of mutating viruses that plague the earth?" What does Jesus do instead? The showdown is in the desert, alone and away from the crowds. And how, the skeptic might ask, is Jesus' power demonstrated before Satan—except to refuse the dare?

If God's silence and hiddenness were supposed to be finally and overcome once-for-all through the incarnate Christ, Jesus did not meet the expectation. Jesus was both visible and invisible. The crowds saw him, but they didn't see him. The disciples and his mother and his brothers recognized him, but they didn't recognize him. He was visible, but at the same time invisible. In *The Ancient Laugh of God*, J. Marshall Jenkins has captured this anomaly under the general heading "Ironies of Presence and Absence." He retells the Gospel stories, effortlessly adding a contemporary flavor: "Mark tells tales of sensational, show-stopping healings, only to have Jesus admonish the crowd to stifle their applause and pretend the show never came to town." In reference to the girl raised from the dead in chapter 5, he continues:

> Instead of just a miracle play, we have high comedy: an itinerant son of a carpenter from a someplace halfway between here and nowhere rambles into town, raises a young girl from the dead, and tells the local news media to shut off their cameras and go fetch her a Big Mac. "Don't mind me. I was just doing my job," Jesus seems to say with a tip of his hat as he rides off into the sunset with his twelve sidekicks.

But the Gospel of Mark also shows a very different turn of events. "Comedy becomes tragedy as the tables turn and Jesus cannot make himself visible to save his life. He returns to the old hometown to teach in the synagogue, only to find that no one pays attention to his message." Here they see him as "just a hometown boy who ought to stay in line and build cabinets"—one of their own. "This invisibility would eventually be the death of him, as the religious authorities in another town, never recognizing their long-awaited Messiah, would have him put to death. . . . He was most visible while trying to stay behind the scenes and most invisible while trying to make himself and his message known."

But what about his miracles? Didn't Jesus break the silence—the sense of absence—through his healings and by changing water into wine? The Gospels are filled with accounts of miracles. The short span of Jesus' ministry stands out amid the whole of biblical history. There were certain periods of supernatural signs, and this was certainly one of them. But was this a time that uniquely revealed the presence of God? Richard Friedman argues that God's presence was strangely absent in the ministry of Jesus. He points out that God's personal interaction beginning with Adam and Eve gradually diminishes through the course of biblical history. To those who would insist that with the coming of Christ we have the ultimate *appearance of God,* Friedman disagrees. While it is true that Jesus, Immanuel—*God with us*—in one sense turns any notion of *disappearance* on its head, there is another sense in which God was hidden in the midst of the incarnation. And Jesus contributed to that sense of hiddenness by, among other things, persistently making reference to himself as the "Son of Man." Yet after centuries with few recorded supernatural signs from God, "one is struck," Friedman concedes, "by the great rush of miracles that one encounters in the Gospels. It is an unparalleled concentration; there has been no portrayal of so many episodes of miracles in so short a time span before."

But most of Jesus' miracles, like those of Elijah and Elisha, are more personal than the spectacular miracles of Moses who parted the Red Sea to escape the Egyptians. Furthermore, some of the miracles were kept secret on the instructions of Jesus himself. And in the end Jesus' miracles do not convince the authorities or the masses that God incarnate has been among them. In the final analysis, belief in Jesus is a matter of faith.

THE CRUCIFIXION

The single most astounding incident that identifies Jesus with the disappearance or silence of God is the crucifixion, and particularly Jesus' last words on the cross—the cry of "Why have you left me?" Here the silence of God is palpable. "Against the background of the divine-human struggle as traced in the Hebrew Bible from the Garden of Eden to the hiding of the face of God," writes Friedman, "the story of the death of Jesus in the New Testament appears as a culmination of that struggle. An incarnation of God moves among humans on earth in the form of a human being, and they kill him."

That Jesus would experience a sense of abandonment is not merely a curious anomaly that we ponder today; rather it is a profound preview of our own response to circumstances that appear utterly devoid of the divine presence. Theologian Jürgen Moltmann suggests that it was not the physical pain—as horrific as it was—but the searing sense of abandonment that was Jesus' worst suffering on the cross. "The suffering in the passion of Jesus is abandonment, rejection by God, his Father." Thus God incarnate *feels* our cry of abandonment. "When God becomes man in Jesus of Nazareth, he not only enters into the finitude of man, but in his death on the cross also enters into the situation of man's godforsakenness." So when we quote Philippians 3:10, "I want to know Christ and the power of his resurrection and the fellowship of sharing in his sufferings," that includes the suffering of abandonment—particularly in times of sorrow and loss.

That Jesus is gloriously resurrected on the third day does not solve the problem of absence—at least for evangelicals. God is no longer walking in the Garden with Adam and Eve, nor is Jesus walking along the Sea of Galilee. For Catholics, however, there is a *real presence* that some of the Reformers rejected. "Instead of being the literal transubstantiation of bread and wine into the body and blood of Christ, the Eucharist came more and more to be seen in the Zwinglian or Calvinistic manner," writes J. Hillis Miller. "To these reformers [though certainly not true of Luther and, to a lesser extent, Calvin] the bread and wine are mere signs commemorating the historical fact that Christ was once, long ago, present on earth: 'This do in remembrance of me.' Instead of being a sharing in the immediate presence of Christ, the communion service became the expression of an absence." Most evangelicals today have accepted the Zwinglian definition of the Lord's Supper, viewing it as a symbolic remembrance of Christ's death.

Miller makes a very thought-provoking observation that the Lord's Supper in all its symbolism and spiritual significance emanates absence. We are eating and drinking to the lifeless body and spilled blood of one who died for our sins. This do in *remembrance* . . .

The Reformation faith, as it has developed since the sixteenth century, has devalued mystery. The Bible alone—*sola scriptura*—is our text. We venerate Bible study with an excessive array of lesson plans, concordances and commentaries. We are uncomfortable with the *unknown* and the *ambiguous*. And in the generations following the Reformation the gap between faith and mystery grew even wider. During the evangelical revivals of the eighteenth century—and the age of Romanticism that followed—sanguine notions of spirituality came to the fore. Jesus became our intimate friend. "Jesus and me in close relation," we sang so casually around the campfire.

The unfathomable mystery of the incarnation became ordinary and mundane, with Jesus in long light-brown hair, donned in sandals and robe, and milling about among the other paper flannel-graph figures. He was a tame Jesus and very predictable. We were not supposed to question: *That's impossible! How can God look like an ordinary white guy? How can he die one day and show up walking through a door a few days later?* The mystery and incomprehensibility were drained right out of our rational and coherent historically based faith. We had no rituals, no holy days, no Mass said in Latin. Ascension Day was not observed. But we had our paper Jesus who could rise right through the puffy paper clouds and over the top of that flannel board. He was surely gone, but we sang with gusto, "He lives, He lives. . . . You ask me how I know he lives, He lives within my heart."

If Jesus is not an ordinary white guy who walks and talks with me, and if he is not the Eucharist wafer distributed by the priest, who then is he? *Who do you say that I am?* Jesus asks us. The right answer, from both the apostle Peter and Martha, the sister of Mary, is "You are the Christ, the Son of God" (Matthew 16:16; John 11:27). But who is this Christ for us today? Dietrich Bonhoeffer, pastor and theologian, repeatedly asked this question. Living in Nazi Germany amid the swirl of Hitler's foreign aggression and domestic terror, he anguished over the condition of religion in his native land—a religion that offered no principled response to the moral corruption of the Third Reich. There had been those who had sought for renewal or revival in Christianity, but not Bonhoeffer. He called for a radical form of discipleship—a "religionless Christianity" or no Christianity at all: "The Christian religion as a religion is not of God. . . . Christ is not a bringer of a new religion, but the bringer of God, therefore as an impossible road from man to God the Christian religion stands with other religions. . . . So the gift of Christ is not the Christian religion, but the mercy and love of God which culminate in the cross."

The question haunted Bonhoeffer: *Who is Christ for us today?* One of his letters smuggled from a Nazi prison sums up his thoughts: "What's bothering me incessantly is the question of what Christianity really is, or indeed who Christ really is, for us today." For him christology was practical and down to earth. Jesus is among us "on the factory floor" or "at a political meeting." He saw Jesus among us as "the least of these" brothers and sisters—a metaphor that he saw most powerfully depicted in the work of a Russian novelist:

Dostoevsky let the figure of Christ appear in Russian literature as

> the idiot. He does not separate himself, but clumsily causes offense everywhere. He does not go around with the great ones, but with children. He is laughed at and loved. He is the fool and he is the wise man. He bears everything and he forgives everything. He is revolutionary and yet he conforms. He does not want to—but he does—call attention to himself just by his existence. Who are you? Idiot or Christ?

When Christ is hidden, disguised as an idiot, how can we find him? The incarnation has come and gone. "I believe the Bible alone is the answer," writes Bonhoeffer. "One must be prepared really to enquire of it. . . . That is because in the Bible God speaks to us. . . . And whoever would find [God] must go to the foot of the Cross. . . . This is the message of the Bible, not only in the New but also in the Old Testament."

HEARING JESUS' VOICE

I wonder if one of the reasons that some people do not find the Bible sufficient as the *voice* of God is that it has become too familiar, whereas the claim to hear an actual voice brings new ideas and new ways to comprehend God. But perhaps the problem is our failure to look at Scripture with an open and fresh perspective. Jesus speaks to us today through the same parables he spoke two thousand years ago. His words alone can bring personality and voice to what otherwise may seem like a distant, silent God. Referring to the parable of the lost sheep and the parable of the "country-club crowd," Frederick Buechner writes: "I think that these parables can be read as jokes about God in the sense that what they are essentially about is the outlandishness of God who does impossible things with impossible people, and I believe that . . . the truth they contain can itself be thought of as comic." Buechner goes on to tell Jesus' parable of the prodigal son as a joke that gives us a glimpse of God. It is a timeless story about God that needs no further punch lines. Easy testimonies of "the Lord told me" cannot improve on the words the Lord has already spoken:

> The Prodigal Son goes off with his inheritance and blows the whole pile on liquor and sex and fancy clothes. . . . He gets a job on a pig farm and keeps at it long enough to observe that the pigs are getting a better deal than he is and then decides to go home. . . . There is no sign that he is sorry for what he's done or that he's resolved to make amends somehow. . . . The old man sees him coming around the corner below the tennis court and starts sprinting down the drive like a maniac. Before the boy has time to get so much as the first word out, the old man throws his arms around him and all but knocks him off his feet with the tears and whiskers and incredulous laughter of his welcome.
>
> The boy is back, that's all that matters. . . . They turn on the stereo. They break out the best Scotch. They roll back the living room carpet and ring up the neighbors.
>
> Is it possible, I wonder, to say that it is only when you hear the Gospel as a wild and marvelous joke that you really hear it at all?

The voice of Jesus rises above all others in Scripture, and it is that voice that brings assurance in times of difficulty. I can understand how someone—perhaps a New Age guru—who views Jesus as a mere man would claim their own words from Jesus. But how could anyone, I wonder, who claims Jesus as Lord and who accepts the Bible as the Word of God, put more words in the mouth of Jesus than he has already spoken. Is it possible to improve on the Sermon on the Mount or the prayer for unity or the parables or the words on the cross? Jesus has spoken, and those words ought to forever ring in our ears as the voice of God.

Buechner offers further insights on listening to God—listening to the voices in Scripture—especially the voice of Jesus. The whole Bible calls us to hear. "But hear what?" he asks. "The Bible is hundreds upon hundreds of voices all calling at once out of the past and clamoring for our attention like barkers at a fair, like air-raid sirens, like a whole barnyard of cockcrows as the first long shafts of dawn fan out across the sky." We listen to all those voices. Whether Moses or Job or Simeon, they demand our attention. But "somewhere in the midst of them all one particular voice speaks out that is unlike any other voice because it speaks so directly to the deepest privacy and longing and weariness of each of us. . . . Come, the voice says. Unto me. All ye. Every last one."

Those generalized words that ought to be received in a very personal way truly are for every last one. But there are other words of Jesus that are even more specific in their compassion—and not words only. The very actions and body language of Jesus speak volumes to us today. I sense this so profoundly as a woman. Having lived for more than a half century in a world where a woman is deemed lesser than a man, I find an advocate in Jesus. He is the one who stands up against the authorities and says, *This is wrong. Woe to you who abuse and corrupt legitimate authority. Your self-righteous arrogance is exposed by my searing gaze.* The Gospel account of Jesus and the woman taken in adultery is a scathing indictment of those in authority. This woman stands in for all women—and others—who have been wounded by a double standard, whether in the home or the church or the workplace. Here the body language of Jesus is palpable. He is a man of authority among men of authority. Those in power have circled the wagons. The woman is vulnerable and defenseless. Jesus stoops down and writes in the sand, perhaps a ploy to divert attention from the woman. Silence. He goads them. He knows the sinful hearts beneath the pretense, the pious and proud exterior. Whatever their sins were, whether adultery or worse, Jesus was on to them. *Be a man,* he taunted. *Step up and throw a stone—if you dare.* They didn't. They walked away, tails between their legs. Jesus turned. "Woman, where are they? Has no one condemned you?" She responded, "No one, sir." His reply rings out with compassion down through the ages. "Neither do I condemn you. Go now and leave your life of sin" (John 8:3-11).

Jesus has weighed in. This is the voice of God on abuse of power. However, throughout history (even today) there has been a temptation for the one who has been mistreated or left alone to claim a special calling or message from God, a personalized word of compassion from God. The one who is stripped of dignity—whether the "lady preacher" or the "witch" or the "uppity" woman—hears a voice. Perhaps. But God, through the incarnate Jesus, has already spoken words that heal a wounded spirit: *Neither do I condemn you.*

Truly the voice of Jesus rises above all others in Scripture. But it also rises above all other voices that have ever spoken—above all other prophets of the world's religions. And the message is singular. Jesus has spoken once for all in that short window of time to show us who God is. To be sure, the mystery remains, but the incarnate Christ revealed God, very God. Dutch theologian and missiologist Johan Herman Bavinck summed up this powerful truth succinctly: "Man has thought that God was like the silent, impersonal, primeval ocean, or like a great fire in which we, like sparks, fly up for a moment only to fall back again when our existence comes to an end. But in . . . Jesus Christ alone, the *Logos,* the Word, we hear His voice and see His image."

In *Encounters with Silence,* Karl Rahner offers a prayer to God that confesses his deep longing and search for God: "When I try to take You into account in the calculations of my life," he laments, "I can only put You down as an 'unknown'—the riddle of Your Infinity, which Itself contains everything, throws all my calculations off, and so the end result is still an insoluble puzzle." He then counsels God: "You must make Your own some human word, for that's the only kind I can comprehend." Then there is recognition that this is the very thing that God has already done:

> O Infinite God, You have actually willed to speak such a word to me. You have restrained the ocean of Your Infinity from flooding

> in over the poor little wall which protects my tiny life's acre from Your Vastness. Not the waters of Your great sea, but only the dew of Your Gentleness is to spread itself over my little plot of earth. You have come to me in a human word. . . .
>
> Grant, O Infinite God, that I may ever cling fast to Jesus Christ, my Lord.

Emanuel, God with us, is the powerful message of the incarnation of Jesus. "If the poetry of Jesus' message has anything to commend it," writes Michael Frost, "it's that God has once and for all drawn near and will never again retreat from this world." Frost, a writer and educator from Australia, tells an interesting story about a Nativity service at a church near Sydney, in which he was the invited speaker:

> It was a dusty hall, and we perched on precarious folding metal chairs. Children enacted the Christmas story and a ventriloquist worked his magic. Then at one point in the meeting a young woman with a huge voice arrived on stage and started belting out the Bette Midler song, "From a Distance" . . . "God is watching us from a distance." It did not seem like an appropriate song for Christmas. But then suddenly a woman in the audience joined the soloist, singing her own words—in a challenge of sorts: "God came near to us, God came near to us, God came near to us, at Christmas." It was a powerful advent message—especially for people who comprehend Bette Midler's song far more easily than they do the incarnation.

HOW SILENTLY, HOW SILENTLY

Is Jesus talking with us today? Some people cannot live without a message directed exclusively for themselves in words they can repeat. Jesus, they reason, is not fulfilling his role if he is not speaking words today that were not spoken two thousand years ago. But a talking Jesus—one who voices our own words—is surely no improvement over the Jesus who lived and walked and talked among us. "Jesus told me. Jesus said to me." These are phrases we dare not use. Hearing those words was the unique privilege of only a small number of people who lived during a short period of time. The one exception was the apostle Paul. As Saul, the great persecutor of Christians, he was stopped dead in his tracks, blinded by a light and verbally accosted by the voice of Jesus. This decisive incident set the stage for him to become an apostle. It is no small matter for someone else to claim a similar encounter. Fabricating conversation is a serious transgression. But more than that, it diminishes the greatest event of history: the incarnation, when God became man. If we truly believe and honor that most precious doctrine, we will avoid the temptation of giving words to our risen Lord. His words were astonishing. They are memorable, and they ought to live in our hearts. We cannot improve on them, and to attempt to do so is not only presumptuous but it is trifling with what is holy.

When I think of the words of Jesus for us today, I immediately think of his words in the Gospels. But I believe there are also silent words that need no language or sound to be conveyed for those who will hear. These are the silent words that a good friend of mine heard years ago after the drowning death of his two-year-old son Danny. The person who brought him the greatest consolation in the dark days that followed was a friend who came to his house and said, "Let's go for a walk." They walked and walked, block after block, hour after hour, it seemed. The friend said not a word. No conversation passed between them. There were no words that could improve on the silence. So it is with Jesus.

How silently, how silently
The wondrous gift is given.

10

"THIS IS MY FATHER'S WORLD"

God Beyond the Beyond

This is my Father's world,
and to my listening ears
all nature sings, and round me rings
the music of the spheres. . . .

This is my Father's world:
he shines in all that's fair;
in the rustling grass I hear him pass;
he speaks to me everywhere.

MALTBIE D. BABCOCK, "THIS IS MY FATHER'S WORLD"

Reformed theology recognizes two related, though separate and distinct, forms of God's revelation: special and general, the Bible and the so-called book of nature. John Calvin articulated this concept, and others since his time have refined and expanded this dual aspect of God's self-disclosure. The Bible shows us a personal God concerned with creation, especially humankind. Nature shows us God's grandeur and design. Each supports the other. The Bible provides a written record, and its truthfulness is something we accept by faith. That Moses parted the Red Sea and that Jesus walked on water are incidents I would not expect non-Christian historians to believe. But the book of nature opens her pages for all to read with awe and wonder. Yet it is that very book that troubles many people—Christians and non-Christians alike.

While many Christians speak of deepened faith when looking into the heavens on a starry night, others, myself included, are unable to fathom the distance between ourselves and the God who set this universe in motion. As much as we may want to believe otherwise, this vast distance intertwined with time continually challenges our belief in God. That there is a personal God who transcends time and space is a concept that I cannot fathom with my intellect alone. Indeed, the billions and billions of light years are a constant reminder that my belief in God rests on faith.

For many people, however, this distance is translated into absence, and faith does not suffice. For some of them, life without God seems to progress without a hitch. But for others, there is a sense of hopelessness and meaninglessness. They hear of faith deeply felt by others, but for them there is no divine presence. Feigning faith is not a solution. Their lament is not the lament of sorrow that a parent experiences at the death of a child or a spouse. It is rather a haunting awareness of a distant God who has withdrawn his presence, if in fact God ever was truly present. It is the regret of Emily Dickinson—the lament that God hides "his rare life from our gross eyes." It is the sadness of a forlorn wayfarer or a child left behind, lost and alone in the desert calling for her mother. "The silence of God, the unbearable silence of God." These were the words used by Dominique de Menil to describe a series of paintings on panels in the Rothko Chapel in Houston, paintings that evoke "the tragic mystery of our perishable condition."

It is a tragedy when for some people the silence and distance of God becomes unbearable, and for no fault of their own. They are often the most God-intoxicated and God-obsessed among us, but for them faith does not come easily or does not come at all. They surely do not possess what the Bible speaks of as the *gift* of faith. They are the ones of whom

Martin Marty writes of in his book *A Cry of Absence*. For them "God is silent." They possess a "wintery sort of spirituality." They find their habitation not in a lush summery spirituality but rather on the "barren wintery landscape where the January thaw may provide some respite"—but often only for a short duration before they hunker down again amidst what often seems like an eternal February chill.

For most people who sense the silence of God, however, silence is not the central issue. These folks would never lament the silence of God when the sun is shining and they are surrounded by successful adult children and healthy and playful grandchildren. God's silence affects them only when circumstances seem to require a God not so much of words but of action. God's silence becomes unbearable when that sunny day turns into a nightmare—when the little one is pulled beneath the waves in the undertow.

The ultimate symbol of the unbearable silence of God—especially in Jewish literature—is the Holocaust. But it is important to point out here as well that *silence* is not really the characteristic of God that is on trial. Rather it is inaction. No words could ameliorate the unspeakable atrocities of the Holocaust—only action. And God, it was perceived, neither acted nor spoke.

Words and actions, though, are often closely connected by those who emphasize God's immediate and supernatural involvement in our lives today. God is portrayed as not only having intimate conversations with those who are listening but also as performing miracles, signs and wonders for those who are asking. Such testimonials, however, ring hollow to those who have endured the Holocaust or terrible tragedy on a lesser scale. When God is regarded as a close buddy and bighearted benefactor, disillusionment easily sets in when we are face to face with a tragedy or even a job loss. Who is this one with whom I am having intimate conversations? What are the "attributes" of this God? Uncaring? Impotent? Angry? Insincere? Unfair? Inattentive?

THE TWO BOOKS

So how then do we develop a relationship with God who is sovereign over the good times as well as the bad? Who is this One who holds the whole world in his hands in both sunshine and rain? How do we relate in a personal way with our Father who art in heaven—the very One who set the big bang in motion? Bottom line, can anyone really know God across the span of time and distance?

The simple answer is that we know God through the revelation of Scripture. The more we read, the reasoning follows, the more familiar we become with this larger-than-life personage. But that is not necessarily true. Theologians and students of Scripture often confess that the more they learn of God, the less they really know. And recent attempts to write a biography of God based on the Bible do not solve the problem.

That Scripture also shows us God through the incarnate Son is not an insignificant detail. Indeed, this offers the most intimate portrait in the biography. But even then God is mysterious—though arguably less so than God revealed through the third person of the Trinity, the Holy Spirit. And so, the biography of God still seems incomplete. The best we can do is to write an addendum ourselves, written on our hearts and rewritten every day of our lives. The temptation of some, however, is to turn this final section into a second book that stands alongside the Bible. Here God is prominently featured, but only secondarily to ourselves. Mystery is substituted for dialogue and description. The blurred portraits are replaced by sharp photos. This book, however, is our own book and should never be confused with the revelation of Scripture.

Amid the absorption of writing this autobiographical volume, the second book of God, the book of nature (which offers a lifetime of chapters and verses to explore) is often neglected. This book for me, with all its hidden mysteries and ironies, has become a treasured companion volume to the Bible. Like the Bible, it often puzzles me, but in its unanswered questions I love it all the more. Indeed, through this two-volume set, God's silent voice echoes through the light years of space even as it filters into my heart through the pages of Scripture.

Finding God in nature is not purely a pastime for pantheists. The Bible begins with a declaration of God's creation, and from the psalms to the parables we find both appreciation and awe. But beyond the Bible and our own communion with nature, our spiritual lives are nourished by what artists and poets and mystics have brought to the Lord's Table. Here the silent voice of God whispers even as it roars and thunders.

One who has powerfully captured this voice of God in creation is the Dutch Renaissance man—pastor, theologian, social activist, newspaper publisher, educator, prime minister, husband and father—Abraham Kuyper. He could be described as a *superman*—by either the philosophical or popular usage of that term. Yet amid his hectic life, he struggled with depression. On one occasion, shortly after a retreat in the Swiss Alps to recover from a breakdown, he wrote a prayer meditation titled "In the Roar of Your Waterfalls," based on Psalm 42:7:

> Deep calls to deep
>   in the roar of your waterfalls;
> all your waves and breakers
>   have swept over me.

Kuyper didn't originally publish it in an obscure devotional book but for public consumption in his newspaper. Here he suggests that we must get away from the hustle and bustle of life and go to the mountains, where God's silent voice speaks in the roar of the waterfall:

> God the Lord did not give us His revelation in a land of plains but in a land with mountains. Only in these highlands does a person learn to understand many a saying in Scripture. . . .
>
> On the plains and in the valleys man is everything. There he builds his cities and towns and fills them with his worldly posses-

> sions. There he accumulates his wealth, creates his pleasures, and covers the earth with the works of his hands.
>
> But on mountain heights the picture is very different. There man is the creator of nothing and God alone is the majestic master craftsman. There every peak, every cliff, every gorge is an eloquent witness to His divine greatness. . . .
>
> Silence, a sacred silence, fills the air over those mysterious highlands. There the pounding of hoofbeats, the rattle of implements, the buzz of human voices is never heard but everything lies wrapped in solemn and divine quiet. . . . One hears only a muffled, regular, heavenly roar, a voice of God, the roar of the waterfalls of the Almighty.
>
> For David, the servant of God, the voice of God in those plunging waters was full of holy poetry: they mediated to him the sacred presence of God.

I too have heard the voice of God in the waterfall. In fact, when I first read this meditation, it reminded me of a time when my *waterfall spirituality* was challenged by a student. I was teaching a course on cults and the New Age, and our discussion was on meditation. The students all agreed that meditation on Scripture was a good practice for a Christian, but I pushed them beyond that. I told them of my special love for waterfalls and how I often seek out falls when I travel—whether in northern Wisconsin, the Upper Peninsula of Michigan, the Finger Lakes, Yellowstone, Yosemite or my favorite spot, Silver Falls State Park. Here in a rain forest in the lower elevation of the Cascade Mountains of Oregon, I spent an afternoon on Canyon Trail that features ten scenic waterfalls, bordered by ferns, moss, wildflowers and trees of biblical proportion: fir, hemlock and cedar. With Silver Falls fresh on my mind, I told my students how I visualize the majesty of the waterfalls when I feel stressed. I close my eyes and feel and hear the water splashing over my forehead, even as I did under one of the falls on the Canyon Trail. A student immediately asked, "Did you meditate on God's Word when you were doing that?" I responded, "No. I just felt and heard the waterfall." He insisted that such a mindless form of meditation was opening up myself to the power of Satan.

I recently heard the voice of God cascading down Cataract Falls in the Colorado Rockies, and as I listened I was reminded of Luci Shaw's references to the voice of God in nature. She also speaks of finding God in the landscape—not the nature god of pantheism or the demonic spirits of spiritualism but the very God we find in the psalms. "When I breathe into my lungs the spiced sharpness of morning mist moving across our Pacific Northwest lake," she writes, "I am reminded of *the air of prayer.* When I look up at looming, capped-with-snow Mt. Baker, with its signature wisp of vapor, I wonder, 'Is this a metaphor for *God-strength, God-presence?*' The thundering rattle of breakers on the pebbled shore of Puget Sound enters my ears like an echo of what God's voice might sound like."

So too it was for me in hearing the roar of the waters of Cataract Falls. I'm convinced we can hear the silent voice of God in nature, though surely not if we are too fearful of Satan, as my student was. Neither Kuyper nor Shaw nor the psalmist were afraid of the voice of God in nature, though these experiences are not the nuts and bolts of life. Kuyper reminds us (having endured dark depression himself) that there is also darkness on the mountains and in the roar of the waterfall—but even in the darkness, God is there:

> Still, it is not in the mountains but on the plains that God provided a home for humanity. Though a person might roam on mountain heights, he could not live there, and after years of being tested David, too, returned to the plain of the Jordan. But the memory of his God as he received it in God's mountains remained indelibly imprinted on his soul. . . . Sometimes the scene on those moun-

> tains becomes especially impressive. The sky grows dark and the clouds stack up and the rains come down in torrents that you never see on the plains. . . . But in the midst of that darkness the voice of the waters swells in power and majesty. . . .
>
> David carried down a memory from these awful moments for us, too. For in our life too a fearful somberness often overcomes us. Everything becomes dark. . . . It may come from suffering and misfortune. It may come from deep anxiety and inner distress. But whatever the cause, a child of God, listening amidst that somberness, also hears the mounting sound of the voice of God. The Lord Himself is in that darkness.

God's silence is not something that we ought to merely accept or endure. The silence is our refuge. We can find solace in the silence of God. Should not we therefore celebrate the silence of God—or if not *celebrate* it, at least *cultivate* it as part of our spiritual sojourn? Barbara Brown Taylor offers insights as she captures the essence of Max Picard's poetic eulogy, *The World of Silence:* "Picard says that silence is the central place of faith, where we give the Word back to the God from whom we first received it. . . . In silence, we travel back in time to the day *before* the first day of creation, when all being was still part of God's body. It had not yet been said, and silence was the womb in which it slept."

If this reminds us of some of the incomprehensible poetry we encountered in our high school English literature class, perhaps it needs another reading—and then an assault on the original source. But Picard is in some ways as scientific as he is spiritual and poetic. The silence of God is intrinsically bound to the incomprehensible vastness of the universe, a vastness that is essentially one and the same as *time.* To travel back in time to the day before creation is to find God in silence and God in pure form and singular essence without the wonder and the complicated messiness of creation.

Contemplating God at a time before creation relates to the mystery of God's very identity. We ask again, *Who* is God? Does anyone really know who God is? When forced to identify God, Christians easily come up with an infinite number of descriptions. They are like eyewitnesses to a crime. Each witness describes the suspect differently. Bottom line, it is often very difficult to identify the suspect—God, the suspect. The description of one witness sometimes conflicts with the description of another. Friedman puts this in perspective as it relates to the other gods in the Bible:

> From the beginning of the book to the end, the essence of God remains unknown. Shamash is the sun. Baal is the storm wind. Asherah is fertility. Yamm is the sea. But what is Yahweh? Residing outside of nature, known only through words and through acts in history, God in the Bible remains a mystery. The stuff of Yamm is the sea waters, but what is the "stuff" of the God of the Bible? Even when God in the Bible is most intimately known to humans—in the garden of Eden, at the revelation at Sinai—they are not privileged with an iota of knowledge of the substance of God. . . . The most that humans are allowed to know is the outward personality of Yahweh: a merciful and gracious God, long-suffering, abundant in kindness. . . . But what Yahweh *is* is the Bible's unspoken, pervasive mystery.

The argument is often made that God is silent because we fail to listen, and that God is hidden because we hide from God. Perhaps. But we take on an unnecessary burden and unwarranted guilt if we only blame ourselves. It is impossible to believe in the God of the Bible and the God of all nature—silent or not—without faith, and faith truly is a gift from God. But even *faith* is a difficult concept to grasp. It is a religious notion fundamental to Christianity alone. Animists do not exercise faith to believe in the spirit world; nor are the gods of the other world religions known primarily through faith. "What's so great about 'faith,'" demanded theologian Greg Boyd's unbelieving father. Why would God not give us an "*obvious* revelation"?

Those questions have been asked a million times, and there is no satisfactory answer. Why is there no obvious revelation in either the Bible or nature? Why do so many people reject these books as authentic portraits of God? Why is God silent? Why is God hidden? Why is belief tied to an exercise of faith? "The world hides God from us, or we hide ourselves from God, or for reasons of his own God hides himself from us," writes Frederick Buechner, "but however you account for it, he is often more conspicuous by his absence than by his presence, and his absence is much of what we labor under and are heavy laden by."

It may be, however, that amid silence we are most attuned to God. When we think we know God or hear God's voice or know God's will, we may actually be the lowest on the bell curve of the cosmic grading system. Those who imagine themselves being first in line with God may actually be last. When God is stripped of mystery, we are left with a god of our own fashioning, perhaps no more than a generous landlord or benefactor.

Annie Dillard, in what might be called vintage Dillard literary form, offers a stream of consciousness worth contemplating—a stream that challenges our overconfidence and our sometimes too secure certainties: "We are most deeply asleep at the switch when we fancy we control any switches at all," she writes. "We sleep to time's hurdy-gurdy; we wake, if we ever wake, to the silence of God. And then, when we wake to the deep shores of light uncreated, then when the dazzling dark breaks over the far slopes of time, then it's time to toss things, like our reason, and our will; then it's time to break our necks for home."

GOD OF THE GAPS

Should it surprise us that we vulnerable human beings are prone to bring God down to our level when God seems so dreadfully far away?

Who can possibly comprehend the cosmos? Not even the best scientists. A recent headline reported that "Hubble Gives First View of Earliest Galaxies." With this telescope we are now looking at an "empty" spot beyond the beyond, in what is called the "Hubble Deep Field"—getting a glimpse of time when the universe was "in its infancy." To many people, such news is scary. The telescope is probing places reserved for God alone. Seeing the universe in its infancy, we fear, might not reflect well on its Creator. Would this God of the universe be the same one who is our personal Savior?

If we become too engrossed in the book of nature, are we edging too close to the slippery slope that leads to atheism? There are scientists who would essentially say yes. Cosmologist Lee Smolin is convinced that science—in all its various specialties—has proved there is no God: "What ties together general relativity, quantum theory, natural selection, and the new sciences of complex and self-organized systems," he argues, "is that in different ways they describe a world that is whole unto itself, without any need of an external intelligence to serve as its inventor, organizer, or external observer."

Other scientists are more open to the possibility of God, or at least *something* beyond the realm that we know. A 1998 cover story in *Newsweek* proclaimed: "Science Finds God." The god science found, however, was more of a process than a person—a distinction that would not have been lost by the proponents of process theology (simply stated, a theology that sees God as not a noun but a verb). "Everything we know about Nature," writes Henry Strapp, "is in accord with the idea that the fundamental process of Nature lies outside space-time, but generates events that can be located in space-time." Huston Smith emphasizes the significance of this theory as it relates to God: "What runs the show . . . lies outside that show." This, says Smith, "provides us with the first level platform since modern science arose on which scientists and theologians can continue their discussions. For God too resides outside those three perimeters."

But does such science actually bring us closer to God? Does this science bolster our belief that "this is my Father's world"?

Other scientists insist that the evidence for God is more than the existence of an unexplained "process" or "something." They argue that while many phenomena might be explained by evolution and other scientific theories, there are some things that are simply too complex to be explained by anything other than what they call intelligent design. Thus these examples of *irreducible complexities* prove there is a God. Niels Gregersen objects: "God cannot and should not be found in the epistemic gaps left over by the limits of current scientific explanation." The existence of God thus is not explained by the scientific gaps of what is not explainable.

Yet it is tempting for scientifically minded Christians to advance some sort of a god of the gaps. In the face of science and *scientism,* they hold on to a God that they find in the gaps and on the fringes of our daily lives. A God of the gaps is one who brings a person back to health when the doctors say there is no hope. Science and technology can handle virtually everything we need, but if there are some holes here and there, we'll plug them with God. This perspective easily leads to a nature-supernature dichotomy. On the one hand we have the secular, and on the other the sacred.

As is true with the Bible, the book of nature is easily misinterpreted. Both point us to God, but the presence of God remains elusive. God's presence, if indeed we ever truly experience it, is a personal presence that is written on our hearts. This presence in its rarest form is often not something that can be easily explained within the framework of either the Bible or the book of nature. It most often comes unexpectedly and it has no words or solutions or benefits—none other than to confirm the profound reality of God in our lives. Yet God remains elusive and mysterious in the midst of silence.

Several years ago when I was going through a very difficult time of doubt and unbelief, I became acquainted with Charlie, a Lutheran with a solid evangelical creed, though one would never know it listening to him. He was a factory executive (owner, CEO, and triple-shift troubleshooter) and maybe that is why he spoke with what I would term factory lingo. There were expletives to be deleted in almost every sentence he spoke, including almost every sentence that he spoke about God. He talked about God matter-of-factly, in very familiar terms. It was in that tone that he told me the story that more than any other has defined his life and his belief in God.

For certain people, like the biblical Job, bereavement unleashes seething, volcanic anger—in some instances so profound that the individual bitterly walks away from faith. But in other cases people are brought closer to God. This was true for Charlie. He told of the indescribable pain of losing his ten-year-old son Mark in a swimming accident. As a single dad he was so profoundly overcome with grief that he would sometimes spend the night at the mausoleum to "sleep" with Mark so Mark wouldn't be afraid, most memorably one Christmas Eve. Mark was a smart kid (who dreamed of going to Harvard to become a lawyer) and a baseball player who made his baseball-playing dad proud.

The searing pain was still there—on his face and in his voice—when he talked about Mark. God, however, was never blamed. In fact, he commented, "Sure, I've struggled with God, but you know, I've got something in common with God. God's Son died, and so did mine." But there was more to Charlie's story. Heaven was closer because of Mark, and the presence of God was real.

About a year after Mark's death, Charlie told how he was taking a much-needed late afternoon nap. When he woke, he "smelled" Mark, and then he realized he had been dreaming about Mark being right there with him. They were talking and laughing like old times. Mark had assured him that he was doing OK, far more than OK. And he satisfied his dad's most dreaded concern, "Are you afraid?" No. Mark was not afraid at all. He was in a more wonderful place than his dad could even imagine.

So powerful and vivid was this encounter that it seemed to Charlie as though it were something beyond a dream. It almost seemed real. Charlie got up and walked into the kitchen. On the counter were donut crumbs and two empty milk glasses. Strange. He and Mark had not dunked donuts in their milk for more than a year.

A skeptic would scoff. I don't know what to think. But whatever happened that afternoon was something very private and personal to Charlie. I base no *theology* on it. Nor did Charlie. But it's possible that this was a moment in time when the silent voice of God brought comfort to a grieving father. Yet for others there is no such presence. They desperately desire the donut crumbs and they long for a voice, but they hear nothing. All they have to cling to is the silence of God.

Barbara Brown Taylor tells of a man who lost his voice at the time of his wife's death, and that loss for him was symbolic of something more profound. He wondered: "Is God more at home in silence than in word? Is the moment of most profound silence the moment of God's most profound presence?" He was not sure, "But at my wife's bedside," he reflected, "where words were hollow and cries powerless, the strongest, most powerful reality was silence."

EPILOGUE

There is something profound about the sound of a voice. As a professor and writer, the written word is critically important to me, but nothing could ever surpass the sound of a voice. I have sometimes played a little mental game with myself, as I imagine others have, wondering which would be worse: losing my hearing or my sight. Visual stimulation is incredibly important to me—not just for reading and weeding my garden but also for the delight of seeing a quick smile or a Lake Michigan sunset or the snow-capped Colorado Rockies. But I would give up my sight sooner than my hearing, and not just for the sound of music. The sound of a voice—the sound of laughter and the sound of a whisper—is to me one of the most precious possessions of life.

The voice, as we are often reminded by the media these days, is totally unique. Like a fingerprint and DNA, everyone has a distinct, one-of-a-kind voice. I would recognize my son's voice over the phone in a split second, even if it didn't always begin with the predictable "Hi, Mom." And there is no one on the planet who says "Mi Mi" the way Kayla, my nine-year-old granddaughter, does.

I lost two voices this past year. They were voices that never had to identify themselves by name on the phone. Alan Neely's gravelly voice, with a distinct southern accent, was known to many, not just to his students at Princeton Seminary and his colleagues in institutions around the country, but to many people in the Spanish-speaking world. Our lively phone conversations were marked by interruptions of each other as much as by laughter, and they always lifted our spirits. We e-mailed each other often, but it was not the same as the sound of his voice. It is his voice that I miss more than anything else.

Bud Berends had a deep, velvety voice. He was one of the best friends I ever had, but that is what many people say. His was a voice of encouragement, and that's what they all say too. Many years ago, when I was going through a very difficult time in my life, it was Bud's voice that most often brought reassurance. It was the *sound* of his voice, not just the words. The day after he died, I dug out a cassette tape of a reading he had done for our church's praise festival some years ago. The tears flooded down my face as I listened to that deep voice. I passed the tape on to his widow, and the sound of his familiar voice was heard one last time in the packed church sanctuary on that sunny summer morning of his funeral.

Two voices have been stilled, and I will never be quite the same. Oh, what I would give for the sound of those voices on the other end of the phone—just one more time.

The voice is a gift. It belongs to the human species only. And for all the delight it can bring, we do the deity no favor in making unwarranted claims for the *voice of God.* For all the comfort we derive from the written Word of God and for the sense of God's presence, God does not speak with a gravelly Texas accent or even a deep, bass voice. We may want it to be true, but it's not. And all the books and articles and tapes and seminars in the world on *listening* to the voice of God will not make it so.

God is God. As mere creatures we have difficulty with that. We want to worship a golden calf and turn God into our closest buddy. Indeed, it is all too tempting to fashion God in our own image. God is God, and with that recognition we must accept the silence of God.

Truly, we are safe in the silence of God.

NOTES

Introduction

p. 11 "One sticks one's finger": Søren Kierkegaard, *Repetition,* trans. by Walter Lowrie (Princeton, N.J.: Princeton University Press, 1946), p. 114.

pp. 11-12 "a great flood of metaphors and symbols": J. Hillis Miller, *The Disappearance of God* (Cambridge, Mass.: Harvard University Press, 1963), p. 7.

p. 17 "It is a mistake to imagine": Parker Palmer, "Preface (1999)," in *The Active Life* (San Francisco: Jossey-Bass, 1990), p. xi.

Chapter 1: Heaven's Megaphone

p. 19 "America Attacked Iraq": James Glaser, Political Columns, July 31, 2003 <www.jamesglaser.org/2003/p20030731.html>.

p. 20 "*Lord,* I prayed: *Grandma is gone now*": Rebecca Roberts, "What Prayer Can Do," *Guideposts,* January 2003, p. 58.

p. 21 "From the confines of Jerusalem": Robert C. Clouse, "Flowering: The Western Church," in *Eerdmans' Handbook to the History of Christianity,* ed. Tim Dowley (Grand Rapids: Eerdmans, 1977), p. 271.

p. 22 "barbarous [Irish] wretches": Alan Kreider and John H. Yoder, "Christians and War," in *Eerdmans' Handbook to the History of Christianity,* ed. Tim Dowley (Grand Rapids: Eerdmans, 1977), p. 24.

p. 22 Edwards called for "the Concert of Prayer": George M. Marsden, *Jonathan Edwards* (New Haven: Yale University Press, 2003), p. 335.

p. 23 "one of the best-chosen . . . in Europe": Ibid., pp. 313, 338.

p. 23 "Some seem to think forts": Ibid., p. 312.

p. 23 "Princeton professors joined Southern preachers": Timothy Smith, cited in Ruth A. Tucker, "The Book That Shaped a Nation: America's (Mis)Use of Scripture," *Voices,* fall-winter 1983-1984, p. 14.

p. 23 "Here is our policy": Robert Lewis Dabney, cited in ibid.

p. 24 "Go to Kiowa": Carry Nation, *The Use and Need of the Life of Carry A. Nation* (Topeka, Kans.: Stevens, 1909), pp. 130, 133-34.

p. 25 "Is there a reliable guide": Jim Wallis, *Who Speaks for God?* (New York: Delacorte, 1996), pp. 6-8.

p. 26 "What do the words *evangelical Christian* mean to you?": Ibid., p. 10.

p. 26 "Let's . . . take another poll": Ibid., pp. 10, 13, 39.

p. 26 "God speaks for God": Ibid., p. 39.

p. 27 "The story of John Brown will mean little": Franklin B. Sanborn, ed., *The Life and Letters of John Brown* (Boston: n.p., 1885), p. 247.

p. 27 "Waving a letter": Merrill D. Peterson, *John Brown* (Charlottesville: University of Virginia Press, 2002), pp. 57-58.

pp. 28-29 "Friday, as was my practice": Paul J. Hill, "Defending The Defenseless" <www.christianheadlines.com>, a revised version of a paper published in an anthology in the Current Controversies series, *The Abortion Controversy,* ed. Lynette Knapp (San Diego: Greenhaven Press, 2001).

p. 29 "The sooner I am executed": Ron Word, "I Expect a Great Reward in Heaven," *Grand Rapids Press,* September 3, 2003, p. A3.

p. 29 In his book *Warfare Prayer:* C. Peter Wagner, *Warfare Prayer* (Ventura, Calif.: Regal Books, 1992), pp. 13, 19.

p. 30 "At 11:45 that evening": Ibid., p. 22.

p. 30 Generals of Intercession: Ibid., pp. 31, 33.

p. 30 It is a "new concept to the great majority": Ibid., pp. 35, 39, 40-41.

pp. 30-31 Wagner does not disguise the elitism: Ibid., pp. 139, 163-64.

p. 31 I recently read a newpaper article: Theresa D. McClellan, "Moms Urge Leniency: Kenyan Won't Do Time for Traffic Deaths," *Grand Rapids Press,* August 1, 2003, p. D1.

Chapter 2: Mixed Messages

p. 36 "The mission for the accomplishment of God's will": Mose Durst, *To Bigotry, No Sanction* (Chicago: Regnery Gateway, 1984), p. 64.

p. 36 "The marriage covenant covers sins": Rene Noorbergen, *Ellen G. White* (New Canaan, Conn.: Keats, 1972), pp. 472-75.

p. 36 Mrs. White "copied and borrowed almost everything": Walter T. Rea, *The White Lie* (Turlock, Calif.: M & R, 1982), p. 50.

pp. 37-38 "It made no sound," she recounts: Helen Schucman, *A Course in Miracles* (Tiburon, Calif.: Foundation for Inner Peace, 1985), p. 87.

p. 38 "God has been preparing me": Mary Baker Eddy, cited in *The First Church of Christ, Scientist, and Miscellany* (Boston: Christian Science Publishing Society, 1941), p. 115.

p. 38 Josephine Woodbury received more than words from God: Robert Peel, *Mary Baker Eddy* (New York: Holt, Rinehart & Winston, 1971), p. 270.

pp. 38-39 "Neale Donald Walsch isn't claiming to be the messiah": Cover copy of Neale Donald Walsch, *The New Revelations* (New York: Atria Books, 2002), p. 2.

p. 39 "You can choose to live your lives": Ibid., p. 14.

p. 39 "Carried away in spirit": Eusebius, *The Ecclesiastical History of Eusebius Pamphilus* (Grand Rapids: Baker, 1955), p. 196.

p. 40 "Thou hast no right to add anything": Fyodor Dostoyevsky, *The Brothers Karamozov,* trans. Andrew MacAndrew (New York: Bantam, 1981), p. 294.

p. 40 Spectacular visions and revelations: Philip Schaff, *History of the Christian Church: The Middle Ages* (Grand Rapids: Eerdmans, 1979), 5:840-42.

p. 41 "They provided information about what practices": Caroline Bynum, *Christ as Mother* (Berkeley: University of California Press, 1982), pp. 181, 194.

p. 41 Vivid descriptions of purgatory: Henry Osborn Taylor, *The Medieval Mind* (Cambridge, Mass.: Harvard University Press, 1949), pp. 470-71.

pp. 41-42 "And I felt the deep, deep silence": Thomas Merton, *The Seven Storey Mountain,* cited in *Pilgrim Souls,* ed. Amy Mandelker and Elizabeth Powers (New York: Touchstone, 1999), p. 110.

p. 42 "Christ is present": John Leax, "Thomas Merton: Giving Up Everything," in *More than Words,* comp. Philip Yancey (Grand Rapids: Baker, 2002), p. 44.

p. 43 "There was this shadow": Merton, cited in *Pilgrim Souls,* p. 400.

p. 43 "Go preach the gospel": Jerena Lee, *Religious Experiences and Journal* (Philadelphia: Jerena Lee, 1849), pp. 14-17.

p. 44 "While the Spirit of God was saying": Salome Lincoln, cited in Almond Davis, *The Female Preacher* (Providence: Elder J. S. Mowry, 1843), pp. 36-37.

p. 44 "It seemed as if a voice said to me": Catherine Bramwell-Booth, *Catherine Booth* (London: Hodder & Stoughton, 1970), p. 185.

p. 46 "You have never heard the voice of God": G. Campbell Morgan, *How to Live* (Chicago: Moody Press, n.d.), p. 78.

p. 46 "The wife of a prophet": A. W. Tozer, *Wingspread: A. B. Simpson* (Harrisburg: Christian Publications, 1943), p. 87.

Chapter 3: Knowing the Mind of God

p. 49 "The author marshals the irrefutable": D. James Kennedy's endorsement of Lee Strobel's *The Case for Christ* (Grand Rapids: Zondervan, 1998).

p. 49 "Among the progenitors of the new evangelicalism": Doug Frank, "Straitened & Narrowed: Did Singing All Those Happy Gospel Jingles Steal Away My Freedom to Think?" *Books & Culture* 3, no. 6 (November/December 1997): 26.

p. 51 The "Great Pumpkin" objection: "Reformed Epistemology and the Rationality of Religious Belief," Allen Stairs's Philosophy of Religion 236 website <http://brindedcow.umd.edu/236/sennett.html>.

p. 51 "In the case of the argument from evil": Ibid.

p. 52 "In fact, far from being a positive argument": William Lane Craig and Walter Sinnot-Armstrong, *God? A Debate Between a Christian and an Atheist* (New York: Oxford University Press, 2004), pp. 125-26.

p. 53 "One of the things that makes men": Norman L. Geisler and Ronald M. Brooks, *When Skeptics Ask* (Wheaton, Ill.: Victor Books, 1990), pp. 62-63.

p. 54 Irrefutable proofs can be "offensive": John G. Stackhouse Jr., *Humble Apologetics* (New York: Oxford University Press, 2002), pp. xvi, 127-30.

p. 54 The amazing future: George M. Marsden, *Jonathan Edwards* (New Haven: Yale University Press, 2003), p. 335.

p. 55 "17,000 to 1": Ibid., p. 336.

p. 55 "I had to wonder": Ravi Zacharias, *A Shattered Visage* (Grand Rapids: Baker, 1990), p. 126.

p. 56 "Well, then, would a reasonable person": Richard Purtill, *C. S. Lewis's Case for the Christian Faith* (San Francisco: Harper & Row, 1981), p. 132.

p. 57 "Lewis himself was in very low spirits": Victor Reppert, "Taking C. S. Lewis Seriously," *Books & Culture* (September-October 2003), p. 12.

p. 57 A personal and professional blow to Lewis: Ibid.

p. 58 Lewis revised the third chapter: C. S. Lewis, "Rejoinder to Dr. Pittenger," in *Undeceptions* (London: Geoffrey Bles, 1971), p. 145, cited in Steve Lovell, "C. S. Lewis's Case Against Naturalism" <www.myweb.tiscali.co.uk/csphilos/biblio.htm>.

p. 58 "The argument fascinated me": Ibid.

p. 58 For some, defending God is entertainment: Lee Strobel, *The Case for Christ* (Grand Rapids: Zondervan, 1998), pp. 113, 206.

p. 59 "Poetry in the prose-flattened world": Walter Brueggemann, cited in Michael Frost, *Seeing God in the Ordinary* (Peabody, Mass.: Hendrickson, 2000), pp. 6-7.

p. 60 "I remain loyal to His Name": Oswald Chambers, cited in Os Guinness, *God in the Dark* (Wheaton, Ill.: Crossway, 1996), pp. 195, 133.

p. 60 Richard H. Popkin's definition of *fideism:* Richard H. Popkin, "Fideism," in *The Encyclopedia of Philosophy,* ed. Paul Edwards (New York: Macmillan, 1967), 3:201-2.

p. 61 The position of Donald Bloesch: Donald Bloesch, *The Ground of Certainty* (Grand Rapids: Eerdmans, 1971), p. 187.

p. 61 "Forty-seven people entered as nonbelievers": Strobel, *Case for Christ,* p. 206.

p. 62 "I'd beaten the captain of the Yale debating team": Charles Templeton, *Farewell to God* (Toronto: McClelland & Stewart, 1996), p. 14.

p. 62 "How did I come to lose my faith?": Sergei Bulgakov, cited in *Pilgrim Souls,* ed. Amy Mandelker and Elizabeth Powers (New York: Touchstone, 1999), p. 94.

p. 62 The words of C. S. Lewis challenge us: C. S. Lewis, *Poems,* ed. Walter Hooper (New York: Harcourt, Brace & World, 1964), p. 129.

Chapter 4: Sola Scriptura

p. 63 "The Bible Stands": Haldor Lillenas, "The Bible Stands," 1917.

pp. 64-65 "When two voices are given to speak to the church": Herman Bavinck, *Reformed Dogmatics* (Grand Rapids: Baker, 2003), 1:512-27.

p. 65 "The first service that one owes": Dietrich Bonhoeffer, "Life Together," in *Writings on Spiritual Direction by Great Christian Masters*, ed. Jerome Neufelder and Mary C. Coelho (New York: Seabury Press, 1982), pp. 86-87.

p. 66 Calvin on preaching as speaking God's Word: T. H. L. Parker, *John Calvin* (Philadelphia: Westminster Press, 1975), pp. 107-8.

p. 67 "St. Paul expected his hearers to be moved": Roland Allen, *Missionary Methods* (London: World Dominion Press, 1912), p. 99.

pp. 67-68 "My faith has found a resting place": Lidie H. Edmonds, "No Other Plea," 1891.

p. 68 J. I. Packer's warning is fitting: J. I. Packer, *God's Thoughts* (Downers Grove, Ill.: InterVarsity Press, 1981), p. 39.

p. 68 Three false "interpretations of how God speaks": Dallas Willard, *Hearing God* (Downers Grove, Ill.: InterVarsity Press, 1999), p. 58.

p. 69 Bible deism: Jack Deere, *Surprised by the Voice of God* (Grand Rapids: Zondervan, 1996), pp. 251, 252, 256.

p. 71 "God disappears in the Bible": Richard Elliot Friedman, *The Disappearance of God* (Boston: Little, Brown, 1995), p. 7.

p. 71 "Adam and Eve take little responsibility for themselves": Ibid.

pp. 71-72 "Beyond the accounts of divine commands": Ibid., pp. 32, 34.

p. 72 "An area where the orthodox or fundamentalist reader": Ibid., pp. 77, 79.

p. 72 Friedman insists otherwise: Ibid., pp. 97, 101.

p. 73 "God is a gentleman": Christopher Christenson, *God Did Not Ordain Silence* (Plainfield, N.J.: Logos International, 1974), pp. 96-97.

p. 74 Barbara Brown Taylor on Abraham: Barbara Brown Taylor, *When God Is*

Silent (Cambridge, Mass.: Crowley Publications, 1998), p. 63.

p. 75 The sheep "will listen to my voice": Joyce Huggett, *Listening to God* (London: Hodder & Stoughton, 1986), pp. 78-81.

p. 75 "We can never be one hundred per cent certain": Ibid., pp. 140-41.

p. 76 John Paul II: "Show Us O Lord Your Mercy," The Holy See, December 11, 2002 <www.vatican.va/holy_father/john_paul_ii/audiences/2002/documents/hf_jp-ii_aud_20021211_en.html>.

p. 77 "The disappearance of God in the Hebrew Bible": Friedman, *Disappearance of God*, p. 116.

p. 77 "Lo, in the grave he lay": Robert Lowry, "Up from the Grave He Arose," 1862.

p. 78 I found comfort in the old gospel song: Septimus Winner, "Whispering Hope" (1868).

Chapter 5: The "Call"

p. 80 "The key is not to make decisions": Henry Blackaby and Richard Blackaby, *Hearing God's Voice* (Nashville: Broadman & Holman, 2002), pp. 4-5, 150.

p. 81 "The chagrined pastor": Ibid., pp. 7-9.

pp. 81-82 Prayer for the Crystal Cathedral: Priscilla Brandt, *Two-Way Prayer* (Waco, Tex.: Word, 1979), pp. 55-57.

p. 82 "Some people are understandably wary": Blackaby and Blackaby, *Hearing God's Voice,* p. 6.

p. 82 It separates Christians from non-Christians: Ibid., pp. x-xi.

p. 83 Defense of women preachers: John Wesley, *The Letters of the Rev. John Wesley,* ed. John Telford (London: Epworth, 1931), 5:257.

p. 84 "When I was about fourteen": Wendell Berry, *Jayber Crow* (Washington D.C.: Counterpoint, 2000), pp. 42-43.

p. 84 Work in South America among the Colorado Indians: Elisabeth Elliot, *These Strange Ashes* (San Francisco: Harper & Row, 1979), pp. 82-83, 108-9.

p. 85 "I was sure it was God's voice": Mother Teresa, cited in Anne Sebba, *Mother Teresa* (New York: Doubleday, 1998), p. 46.

p. 85 "Snake poised to bite": Ibid., p. 36.

p. 86 "When Jonah received his prophetic call": Eugene Peterson, "The Jonah Syndrome," *Leadership* (summer 1990), p. 40.

p. 86 "Inducted into the pastoral care system": Ibid., p. 41.

p. 87 "There are few things so presumptuous": Gordon T. Smith, *Listening to God in Times of Choice* (Downers Grove, Ill.: InterVarsity Press, 1997), p. 67.

p. 87 "Why would anyone": Peterson, "Jonah Syndrome," p. 40.

p. 89 "My wife and I hadn't": Dave Root, "How to Hear the Voice of God" <www.layhands.com/HowToHearGodsVoice.htm>.

p. 90 "There is no simple method": Smith, *Listening to God,* p. 42.

pp. 90-91 Blueprint and wisdom schools: Ibid., p. 16.

p. 91 Smith criticizes both schools: Ibid., p. 18.

p. 91 "Some people have exaggerated": Ibid., p. 18.

p. 91 "The principle of *friendship with God*": Ibid., p. 19.

p. 91 But again he qualifies: Ibid., p. 20.

pp. 91-92 "We need to learn how to listen": Ibid., pp. 34, 52.

p. 92 Set aside a day: Ibid., p. 76.

p. 92 "Mistaken the voice of their own imagination": John Wesley, "The Witness of the Spirit," in *The Works of John Wesley,* ed. Albert C. Outler (Nashville: Abingdon, 1984), 1:269.

p. 92 The wisdom view: Garry Friesen, *Decision Making and the Will of God* (Portland, Ore.: Multnomah, 1980), pp. 243-44.

p. 93 "One's own feelings": Ibid., pp. 245-49.

p. 93 "Man is condemned to be free": Jean-Paul Sartre, "Existentialism Is a Humanism," *Christian Perspectives on Learning* (Grand Rapids: Calvin College, 1989), p. 94.

p. 94 "If my friend's mother": Leslie Weatherhead, *The Transforming Friendship* (London: Epworth, 1962), pp. 155-56.

Chapter 6: The Rules of Listening

pp. 98-99 "I come to the garden alone": C. Austin Miles, "In the Garden" (1913).

p. 100 "What if there is silence when I pray?": Henry Blackaby and Richard Blackaby, *Hearing God's Voice* (Nashville: Broadman & Holman, 2002), pp. 17, 136, 250.

pp. 100-101 "Learning to recognize God's voice": Ibid., p. 246.

p. 101 "God's silence sends strong messages": Ibid., p. 130.

p. 102 "In my circles": Jack Deere, *Surprised by the Voice of God* (Grand Rapids: Zondervan, 1996), p. 15.

p. 102 "Are you into pornography?": Ibid., pp. 15-16.

p. 103 Three steps for God to speak: Ibid., p. 17.

pp. 103-4 Rhonda and Don: Ibid., p. 18.

p. 105 "Just sit down and relax": James Borst, *A Method of Contemplative Prayer* (Bangalore, India: Asian Trading, 1973), p. 11.

p. 106 "For an hour a week": Joyce Huggett, *Listening to God* (London: Hodder & Stoughton, 1986), pp. 50-51, 196.

p. 106 “I made what seems to me a discovery”: Myrtle Fillmore, cited in James Dillet Freeman, *The Story of Unity* (Unity Village, Mo.: Unity Books, 1978), pp. 47-48.

p. 108 “In the way He chooses”: Can You Hear Him? <www.achievebalance.com/data/voice>.

p. 108 “Our God is vitally concerned with reconciliation”: Peter Lord, *Hearing God* (Grand Rapids: Baker, 1988), p. 136.

p. 109 Listening Prayer Ministries: Dan R. Schlesinger, “Table Talk: Observations & Notes Regarding the Doctrines of Listening Prayer & Inner Healing,” Institute for Biblical Apologetics <http://ibainfo.org/tt/listen.html>.

p. 109 She acknowledges Agnes Sanford: Leanne Payne, *The Broken Image* (Grand Rapids: Baker Book House, 1996), pp. 11, 93.

p. 110 “Sanford once heard the Spirit”: Ibid., p. 134.

p. 111 “What deadens us most”: Frederick Buechner, *Telling Secrets* (San Francisco: HarperCollins, 1991), pp. 104-6.

p. 112 Bees singing the Christmas story: Sue Monk Kidd, *The Secret Life of Bees* (New York: Viking, 2002), pp. 143-44.

Chapter 7: The Prayer Closet

p. 114 “The God of *Guideposts*”: Suzanne Britt, “Carrying the Burden of God’s Silence,” *B&R* (fall 1987), p. 3.

p. 115 “All this woman needed was *rain?*”: Charles Templeton, quoted in Lee Strobel, *The Case for Faith* (Grand Rapids: Zondervan, 2000), p. 14.

pp. 116-17 “Those like myself whose imagination”: C. S. Lewis, *The Four Loves* (New York: Fontana, 1963), p. 128.

p. 118 “I believe in miracle”: E. Stanley Jones, *Song of the Assents* (Nashville: Abingdon, 1979), p. 191.

p. 119 “The biggest secret was money”: Alvyn Austin, “No Solicitation: The China Inland Mission and Money,” in *More Money, More Ministry,* ed. Larry Eskridge and Mark A. Noll (Grand Rapids: Eerdmans, 2000), p. 212.

p. 120 “These stories, repeated endlessly”: Ibid., p. 222.

p. 121 Charles and Lettie Cowman: B. H. Pearson, *The Vision Lives* (Fort Washington, Penn.: Christian Literature Crusade, 1961), pp. 53-55, 99.

p. 121 Temptation to “forsake God for other gods”: Donald W. McCullough, *The Trivialization of God* (Colorado Springs, Colo.: NavPress, 1995), pp. 24-25.

p. 122 “My period had come for prayer”: Emily Dickinson, #564 in *The Poems of Emily Dickinson*, ed. R. W. Franklin (Cambridge, Mass.: Harvard University Press, 1996), 1:534.

p. 122 "Pass me not O gentle Savior": Fanny J. Crosby, "Pass Me Not" (1869).

p. 122 "Suddenly I realized the missing ingredient": Ruth Graham, cited in Dale Hanson Bourke, "Ruth Bell Graham: Tough and Tender Moments," *Today's Christian Woman* (November-December 1991), p. 49.

p. 123 "We invite God into our church meeting": Michael Frost, *Seeing God in the Ordinary* (Peabody, Mass.: Hendrickson, 2000), pp. 13-14.

p. 124 "You say grace before meals": G. K. Chesterton, cited in Martin Wroe, *God: What the Critics Say* (London: Spire, 1992), p. 58.

p. 124 Toscanini at the Grand Canyon: Frost, *Seeing God,* p. 66.

p. 125 "Real prayer is something we learn": Richard J. Foster, *Celebration of Discipline,* rev. ed. (San Francisco: HarperCollins, 1988), pp. 38-39.

p. 126 The "Please God" syndrome: Bill Hybels, *Honest to God?* (Grand Rapids: Zondervan, 1990), p. 20.

p. 126 "If Jabez had worked on Wall Street": Bruce Wilkinson, *The Prayer of Jabez* (Sisters, Ore.: Multnomah Publishers, 2000), pp. 30-31.

p. 128 "Prayer did me in every time": Hybels, *Honest to God?* p. 20.

p. 129 "I never privately worshiped God": Ibid., p. 21.

p. 129 "So what about my life of prayer?": Henri Nouwen, cited in Philip Yancey, *Reaching for the Invisible God* (Grand Rapids: Zondervan, 2002), p. 186.

p. 130 "Dare you mock God?": Dr. and Mrs. Howard Taylor, *Hudson Taylor's Spiritual Secret* (Chicago: Moody Press, 1932), pp. 33-37.

p. 131 "The tragedy regarding intercession": Henry Blackaby and Richard Blackaby, *Hearing God's Voice* (Nashville: Broadman & Holman, 2002), p. 135.

Chapter 8: God in the Hands of an Angry Sinner

p. 133 "Lamentations of God's apparent abandonment": Kelly James Clark, *When Faith Is Not Enough* (Grand Rapids: Eerdmans, 1997), p. 9.

p. 133 "Meanwhile, where is God?": C. S. Lewis, *A Grief Observed* (New York: Seabury Press, 1961), pp. 9, 33.

p. 133 "This God, the God of the book": Arthur Krystal, "Why Smart People Believe in God," *American Scholar* 70 (autumn 2001): 34.

p. 136 "I have a friend who, for many months": Doug Frank, "Straitened & Narrowed: Did Singing All Those Happy Gospel Jingles Steal Away My Freedom to Think?" *Books & Culture* 3, no. 6 (November/December 1997): 26.

p. 137 "In their ministerial anxiety": Barbara Brown Taylor, *When God Is Silent* (Boston: Cowley, 1998), p. 69.

pp. 137-38 Circumstances of Charles Williams: C. S. Lewis, introduction to *Essays*

Presented to Charles Williams, ed. C. S. Lewis (Grand Rapids: Eerdmans, 1966), p. xiii.

p. 138 "Yisrael means wrestling with God": David Wolpe, "Don't Tell Me We Should Not Blame God," Beliefnet.com <www.beliefnet.com/story/87/story_8793_1.html>.

p. 138 "Someone began to recite the Kaddish": Elie Wiesel, *Night* (New York: Penguin, 1987), p. 43.

p. 139 "I believe in the sun": Death camp poem, cited in J. Marshall Jenkins, *The Ancient Laugh of God* (Louisville: Westminster/John Knox Press, 1994), p. 62.

p. 139 "Even in exile and suffering": G. Tom Milazzo, *The Silence and the Protest* (Minneapolis: Fortress, 1992), p. 33.

pp. 139-40 "Even in an absolutely desperate situation": Hans Küng, *Does God Exist?* (London: Collins, 1980), p. 628.

p. 140 "Is it OK to wrestle with God?": Henry Blackaby and Richard Blackaby, *Hearing God's Voice* (Nashville: Broadman & Holman, 2002), p. 255.

p. 141 "In the same hospital room with me": Claire Hahn, cited in Patrick Henry and Thomas F. Stransky, *God on Our Minds* (Philadelphia: Fortress, 1982), pp. 5-6.

p. 141 Tevye, in *Fiddler on the Roof*: Joseph Stein, *Fiddler on the Roof* (New York: Simon & Schuster, 1964), p. 23.

p. 142 "Amazing love! How can it be": Charles Wesley, "And Can It Be That I Should Gain" (1739).

p. 143 "I went to my office and poured": John Mark Hicks, *Yet Will I Trust Him: Understanding God in a Suffering World* (Joplin, Mo.: College Press, 1999).

Chapter 9: "Silent Night, Holy Night"

p. 145 "Silent night": Josef Mohr, "Silent Night" (1816).

p. 145 "How silently": Phillips Brooks, "O Little Town of Bethlehem" (1868).

pp. 146-47 "Why not tackle a few macro-problems": Philip Yancey, *The Jesus I Never Knew* (Grand Rapids: Zondervan, 1995), p. 69.

p. 147 "Instead of just a miracle play": J. Marshall Jenkins, *The Ancient Laugh of God* (Louisville: Westminster/John Knox Press, 1994), pp. 18-21.

p. 148 "The great rush of miracles": Richard Elliot Friedman, *The Disappearance of God* (Boston: Little, Brown), p. 130.

p. 149 "And they kill him": Ibid., p. 133.

p. 149 "Man's godforsakenness": Jürgen Moltmann, *The Crucified God* (London: SCM, 1974), p. 276.

pp. 149-50 "Real Presence of Christ": J. Hillis Miller, *The Disappearance of God* (Cambridge, Mass.: Harvard University Press, 1963), p. 6.

p. 151 "He lives, He lives": Alfred H. Ackley, "He Lives" (1933).

p. 151 Religionless Christianity: Dietrich Bonhoeffer, "Jesus Christ and the Nature of Christianity," in Mary Bosanquet, *The Life and Death of Dietrich Bonhoeffer* (New York: Harper & Row, 1968), p. 73.

pp. 151-52 "Who are you? Idiot or Christ?": Dietrich Bonhoeffer, cited in *A Testament to Freedom,* rev. ed., ed. Geffrey B. Kelly and F. Burton Nelson (San Francisco: HarperCollins, 1995), p. 114.

p. 152 "I believe the Bible alone": Bonhoeffer, cited in Bosanquet, *Life and Death,* p. 110.

p. 153 "The Prodigal Son goes off": Frederick Buechner, *Telling the Truth* (San Francisco: HarperCollins, 1977), pp. 66-68.

pp. 153-54 We listen to all those voices: Frederick Buechner, "A Room Called Remember," in *Disciplines for the Inner Life*, ed. Bob W. Benson and Michael W. Benson (Waco, Tex.: Word, 1985), p. 95.

p. 155 "Man has thought that God": Johan Herman Bavinck, *The Church Between Temple and Mosque* (Grand Rapids: Eerdmans, 1981), p. 205.

p. 155 "When I try to take You into account": Karl Rahner, *Encounters with Silence,* trans. James M. Demske (Westminster, Md.: Newman Press, 1966), pp. 15-17.

p. 156 "It was a dusty hall": Michael Frost, *Seeing God in the Ordinary* (Peabody, Mass.: Hendrickson, 2000), pp. 14-15.

p. 157 "How silently, how silently": Phillips Brooks, "O Little Town of Bethlehem," 1868.

Chapter 10: "This is My Father's World"

p. 158 "This is my Father's world": Maltbie D. Babcock, "This Is My Father's World" (1901).

p. 159 "The unbearable silence of God": Dominique de Menil, cited in Julia Goldman, "A Landscape for Contemplation," *The Jewish Week,* July 11, 2003 <www.thejewishweek.com/news/newscontent.php3?artid=8197&print=yes>.

p. 160 "A wintry sort of spirituality": Martin Marty, *A Cry of Absence* (Grand Rapids: Eerdmans, 1997), pp. 109-10.

p. 162 "God the Lord did not give": Abraham Kuyper, "In the Roar of Your Waterfalls," in *Abraham Kuyper: A Centennial Reader,* ed. James D. Bratt (Grand Rapids: Eerdmans, 1998), pp. 148-53.

p. 164 "When I breath into my lungs": Luci Shaw, "Henri Nouwen: Climbing Toward God," in *More than Words,* comp. Philip Yancey (Grand Rapids: Baker, 2002), p. 53.

p. 164 “Still, it is not in the mountain”: Abraham Kuyper, *Abraham Kuyper,* ed. James D. Bratt (Grand Rapids: Eerdmans, 1998), pp. 148-153.

p. 165 Max Picard’s poetic eulogy: Barbara Brown Taylor, *When God Is Silent* (Boston: Cowley, 1998), p. 33.

p. 166 “From the beginning of the book”: Richard Elliot Friedman, *The Disappearance of God* (Boston: Little, Brown, 1995), p. 117.

p. 166 “What’s so great about faith?”: Gregory Boyd, *Letters from a Skeptic* (Wheaton: Victor, 1994), pp. 119-20.

p. 167 “The world hides God from us”: Frederick Buechner, *Telling the Truth* (San Francisco: HarperCollins, 1977), pp. 42-43.

p. 167 “We are most deeply asleep”: Annie Dillard, cited in *Pilgrim Souls,* ed. Amy Mandelker and Elizabeth Powers (New York: Touchstone, 1999), p. 367.

p. 168 Hubble Deep Field: “Hubble Gives First View of Earliest Galaxies,” *Grand Rapids Press,* November 2, 2003, p. F8.

p. 168 “What ties together general relativity”: Lee Smolin, *The Life of the Cosmos* (New York: Oxford University Press, 1997), p. 194.

p. 168 “What runs the show”: Huston Smith, *Why Religion Matters* (San Francisco: HarperCollins, 2001), p. 176.

p. 169 “Found in the epistemic gaps”: Niels Henrik Gregersen, “From Anthropic Design to Self-Organized Complexity,” in *From Complexity to Life,* ed. Niels Henrik Gregersen (New York: Oxford University Press, 2003), p. 212.

p. 171 “Is God more home in silence than in word?”: Taylor, *When God Is Silent,* p. 72.

SELECT BIBLIOGRAPHY

Allen, Roland. *Missionary Methods: St. Paul's or Ours?* London: World Dominion Press, 1912.

Bakke, Jeannette. *Holy Invitation: Exploring Spiritual Direction.* Grand Rapids: Baker, 2000.

Bavinck, Johan Herman. *The Church Between Temple and Mosque*. Grand Rapids: Eerdmans, 1981.

Benson, Bob W., and Michael W. Benson, eds. *Disciplines for the Inner Life*. Waco, Tex.: Word, 1985.

Berry, Wendell. *Jayber Crow.* Washington, D.C.: Counterpoint, 2000.

Blackaby, Henry, and Richard Blackaby. *Hearing God's Voice*. Nashville: Broadman, 2002.

Bloesch, Donald. *The Ground of Certainty.* Grand Rapids: Eerdmans, 1971.

Bonhoeffer, Dietrich. *The Essential Writings of Dietrich Bonhoeffer.* Rev. ed. Edited by Geffrey B. Kelly and F. Burton Nelson. San Francisco: HarperColllins, 1990.

Bosanquet, Mary. *The Life and Death of Dietrich Bonhoeffer*. New York: Harper and Row, 1968.

Boyd, Gregory. *Letters from a Skeptic*. Wheaton, Ill.: Victor, 1994.

Bramwell-Booth, Catherine. *Catherine Booth: The Story of Her Loves*. London: Hodder & Stoughton, 1970.

Buechner, Frederick. *Telling Secrets*. San Francisco: HarperCollins, 1991.

———. *Telling the Truth: The Gospel as Tragedy, Comedy, and Fairy Tale*. San Francisco: HarperCollins, 1977.

Bynum, Caroline. *Christ as Mother: Studies in Spirituality of the High Middle Ages*. Berkeley: University of California Press, 1982.

Christenson, Christopher. *God Did Not Ordain Silence*. Plainfield, N.J.: Logos International, 1974.

Clark, Kelly James. *When Faith Is Not Enough*. Grand Rapids: Eerdmans, 1997.

A Course in Miracles. Tiburon, Calif.: Foundation for Inner Peace, 1985.

Craig, William Lane, and Walter Sinnot Armstrong. *God? A Debate Between a Christian and an Atheist*. New York: Oxford University Press, 2004.

Crossan, John Dominic. *The Historical Jesus: The Life of a Mediterranean Jewish Peasant*. San Francisco: HarperCollins, 1991.

Deere, Jack. *Surprised by the Voice of God: How God Speaks Today Through Prophecies, Dreams, and Visions.* Grand Rapids: Zondervan, 1996.

Dickinson, Emily. *The Poems of Emily Dickinson*. Edited by R. W. Franklin. Cambridge, Mass.: Harvard University Press, 1996.

Dillard, Annie. *Holy the Firm*. New York: Harper, 1988.

Dostoyevsky, Fyodor. *The Brothers Karamazov.* Translated by Andrew R. MacAndrew. New York: Bantam Books, 1981.

Durst, Mose. *To Bigotry, No Sanction: Reverend Sun Myung Moon and the Unification Church*. Chicago: Regnery Gateway, 1984.

Ecclesiastical History of Eusebius Pamphilus. Grand Rapids: Baker Book House, 1955.

Elliot, Elisabeth. *These Strange Ashes*. San Francisco: Harper & Row, 1979.

Eskridge, Larry, and Mark A. Noll, eds. *More Money, More Ministry: Money and Evangelicals in Recent North American History.* Grand Rapids: Eerdmans, 2000.

First Church of Christ, Scientist, and Miscellany. Boston: Christian Science Publishing Society, 1941.

Foster, Richard J. *Celebration of Discipline: The Path to Spiritual Growth*. Rev. ed. San Francisco: HarperCollins, 1988.

Freeman, James Dillet. *The Story of Unity.* Unity Village, Mo.: Unity Books, 1978.

Friedman, Richard Elliot. *The Disappearance of God: A Divine Mystery.* Boston: Little, Brown, 1995.

Friesen, Garry. *Decision Making and the Will of God: A Biblical Alternative to the Traditional View.* Portland: Multnomah, 1980.

Frost, Michael. *Seeing God in the Ordinary: A Theology of the Everyday.* Peabody, Mass.: Hendrickson, 2000.

Geisler, Norman L., and Ronald M. Brooks. *When Skeptics Ask*. Wheaton, Ill.: Victor Books, 1990.

Gregersen, Niels Henrik, ed. *From Complexity to Life: On the Emergence of Life and Meaning*. New York: Oxford University Press, 2003.

Guinness, Os. *God in the Dark: The Assurance of Faith Beyond a Shadow of Doubt*. Wheaton, Ill.: Crossway Books, 1996.

Henry, Patrick, and Thomas F. Stransky. *God on Our Minds*. Philadelphia: Fortress, 1982.

Hicks, John Mark. *Yet Will I Trust Him: Understanding God in a Suffering World*. Joplin, Mo.: College Press, 1999.

Huggett, Joyce. *Listening to God*. London: Hodder & Stoughton, 1986.

Hybels, Bill. *Honest to God? Becoming an Authentic Christian*. Grand Rapids: Zondervan, 1990.

Jenkins, J. Marshall. *The Ancient Laugh of God: Divine Encounters in Unlikely Places*. Louisville, Ky.: Westminster/John Knox Press, 1994.

Jones, E. Stanley. *Song of the Assents*. Nashville: Abingdon, 1979.

Kidd, Sue Monk. *The Secret Life of Bees*. New York: Viking, 2002.

Kierkegaard, Søren. *Repetition*. Translated by Walter Lowrie. Princeton, N.J.: Princeton University Press, 1946.

Kuyper, Abraham. *Abraham Kuyper: A Centennial Reader*. Edited by James D. Bratt. Grand Rapids: Eerdmans, 1998.

Lee, Jerena. *Religious Experiences and Journal*. Philadelphia: Jerena Lee, 1849.

Lewis, C. S. *The Four Loves*. New York: Fontana, 1963.

———. *A Grief Observed*. New York: Seabury Press, 1961.

———. *Poems*. Edited by Walter Hooper. New York: Harcourt, Brace & World, 1964.

Lord, Peter. *Hearing God*. Grand Rapids: Baker, 1988.

Marsden, George M. *Jonathan Edwards: A Life*. New Haven: Yale University Press, 2003.

Marty, Martin . *A Cry of Absence: Reflections for the Winter of the Heart*.Grand Rapids: Eerdmans, 1997.

McCullough, Donald W. *The Trivialization of God: The Dangerous Illusion of a Manageable Deity*. Colorado Springs: NavPress, 1995.

Merton, Thomas. *The Seven Storey Mountain*. New York: Harcourt Brace, 1948.

Milazzo, G. Tom. *The Protest and the Silence: Suffering, Death, and Biblical Theology.* Minneapolis: Fortress, 1992.

Miller, J. Hillis. *The Disappearance of God: Five Nineteenth-Century Writers.* Cambridge, Mass.: Harvard University Press, 1963.

Moltmann, Jürgen. *The Crucified God.* London: SCM, 1974.

Noorbergen, Rene. *Ellen G. White: Prophet of Destiny.* New Canaan, Conn.: Keats Publishing, 1972.

Packer, J. I. *God's Thoughts.* Downers Grove, Ill.: InterVarsity Press, 1981.

Palmer, Parker. *The Active Life: A Spirituality of Work, Creativity, and Caring.* San Francisco: Jossey-Bass, 1990.

Parker, T. H. L. *John Calvin.* Philadelphia: Westminster Press, 1975.

Payne, Leanne. *The Broken Image: Restoring Personal Wholeness Through Healing Prayer.* Grand Rapids: Baker, 1996.

Pearson, Benjamin Harold. *The Vision Lives: The Life Story of Mrs. Charles E. Cowman.* Fort Washington, Penn.: Christian Literature Crusade, 1961.

Peel, Robert. *Mary Baker Eddy: The Years of Trial.* New York: Holt, Rinehart & Winston, 1971.

Peterson, Merrill D. *John Brown: The Legend Revisited.* Charlottesville: University of Virginia Press, 2002.

Purtill, Richard. *C. S. Lewis's Case for the Christian Faith.* San Francisco: Harper & Row, 1981.

Rahner, Karl. *Encounters with Silence.* Translated by James M. Demske. Westminster, Md.: Newman Press, 1966.

Rea, Walter T. *The White Lie.* Turlock, Calif.: M & R Publications, 1982.

Sanborn, Franklin B., ed. *The Life and Letters of John Brown, Liberator of Kansas, and Martyr of Virginia.* Boston: Roberts Brothers, 1885.

Schaff, Philip. *History of the Christian Church: The Middle Ages.* Grand Rapids: Eerdmans, 1979.

Sebba, Anne. *Mother Teresa: Beyond the Image.* New York: Doubleday, 1998.

Smith, Gordon T. *Listening to God in Times of Choice: The Art of Discerning God's Will.* Downers Grove, Ill.: InterVarsity Press, 1997.

Smith, Huston. *Why Religion Matters: The Fate of the Human Spirit in an Age of Disbelief.* San Francisco: HarperCollins, 2001.

Smolin, Lee. *The Life of the Cosmos.* New York: Oxford University Press, 1997.

Stackhouse, John, Jr. *Humble Apologetics: Defending the Faith Today.* New York: Oxford University Press, 2002.

Stein, Joseph. *Fiddler on the Roof*. New York: Simon and Schuster, 1964.

Strobel, Lee. *The Case for Christ: A Journalist's Personal Investigation of the Evidence for Jesus.* Grand Rapids: Zondervan, 1998.

———. *The Case for Faith: A Journalist Investigates the Toughest Objections to Christianity.* Grand Rapids: Zondervan, 2000.

Taylor, Barbara Brown. *When God Is Silent*. Boston: Cowley, 1998.

Taylor, Henry Osborn. *The Medieval Mind.* Cambridge, Mass.: Harvard University Press, 1949.

Taylor, Howard, Dr. and Mrs. *Hudson Taylor's Spiritual Secret*. Chicago: Moody Press, 1932.

Templeton, Charles. *Farewell to God: My Reasons for Rejecting the Christian Faith*. Toronto: McClelland & Stewart, 1996.

Tozer, A. W. *Wingspread: A. B. Simpson: A Study in Spiritual Altitude*. Harrisburg, Penn.: Christian Publications, 1943.

Wagner, C. Peter. *Warfare Prayer.* Ventura, Calif.: Regal Books, 1992.

Wallis, Jim. *Who Speaks for God?* New York: Delacorte Press, 1996.

Walsch, Neale Donald. *The New Revelations: A Conversation With God*. New York: Atria Books, 2002.

Weatherhead, Leslie. *The Transforming Friendship*. London: Epworth, 1962.

Wesley, John Wesley. *The Letters of the Rev. John Wesley.* 8 vols. Edited by John Telford. London: Epworth, 1931.

Wilkinson, Bruce. *The Prayer of Jabez*. Sisters, Ore.: Multnomah Publishers, 2000.

Willard, Dallas. *Hearing God: Developing a Conversational Relationship with God*. Downers Grove, Ill.: InterVarsity Press, 1999.

Wroe, Martin. *God: What the Critics Say.* London: Spire, 1992.

Yancey, Philip. *The Jesus I Never Knew.* Grand Rapids: Zondervan, 1995.

———. *More than Words.* Compiled by Philip Yancey. Grand Rapids, Baker, 2002.

———. *Reaching for the Invisible God.* Grand Rapids: Zondervan, 2000.

Zacharias, Ravi. *A Shattered Visage: The Real Face of Atheism*. Grand Rapids: Baker, 1990.

Index